Scandal

Scandal
The Catholic Church and Public Life

Angela Senander

Foreword by
James A. Coriden, JCD, JD

LITURGICAL PRESS
Collegeville, Minnesota

www.litpress.org

Cover design by Ann Blattner. Illustration: Valueline/Thinkstock.

Excerpts from documents of the Second Vatican Council are from *Vatican Council II: Volume 1, The Conciliar and Post Conciliar Documents*, by Austin Flannery, OP © 1996 (Costello Publishing Company, Inc.). Used with permission.

Scripture texts in this work are taken from the *New Revised Standard Version Bible: Catholic Edition* © 1989, 1993, Division of Christian Education of the National Council of the Churches of Christ in the United States of America. Used by permission. All rights reserved.

Published in the United States of America by Liturgical Press, Collegeville, Minnesota 56321

1   2   3   4   5   6   7   8   9

Library of Congress Cataloging-in-Publication Data

Senander, Angela.
    Scandal : the Catholic Church and public life / Angela Senander.
        p. cm.
    Includes bibliographical references (p.   ) and index.
    ISBN 978-0-8146-3410-3 — ISBN 978-0-8146-3411-0 (e-book)
    1. Catholic Church.   2. Freedom of information in the church.
3. Church and the world.   I. Title.

BX891.3.S46   2012
282—dc23   2012006261

With gratitude to my parents, Robert and Zita Senander,
who shared the gift of faith with me

&

In appreciation of Father James Barry and Father Kevin
Burke, SJ, who led Our Lady of Grace beyond scandal

Contents

Foreword

"Scandal" and "scandalous" are terms frequently invoked but little understood. They are words fraught with ambiguity, realities that are shocking to some and irrelevant to others. The root meanings, "snare," "obstacle," and "stumbling block," reveal the general sense of what a scandal is, but the actual meaning often remains obscure. Hence the reason for this book and the importance of the argument that it makes. It is truly needed and provides a very helpful analysis.

Scandals beyond the Scandal could have been the title of this book. It searches beyond the clergy sexual abuse scandal, the great scandal of our time for the Roman Catholic Church, to look at many, many other scandals, both historical and contemporary, involving the church.

The author is not a scandalmonger, however; she does not tell the stories of dozens of scandalous occurrences in order to spread the word about disgraceful wrongdoing. Far from it; rather, she analyzes the nature of scandal, its elements and ramifications, its diverse meanings, in a wide variety of settings. What is a scandal to some is a perfectly legitimate course of action to others.

Dr. Senander explores the scandalous events in the life of Jesus, in the teachings of the apostle Paul, in the writings of Thomas Aquinas, and in the studies of such moralists as Alphonsus Ligouri, Francis Kenrick, Bernard Häring, and Charles Curran. She looks into actions of individuals within the church, both virtuous and vicious, as well as the church's positions in the "public square," those policy issues, from contraception to immigration, from peacemaking to economic justice, that give rise to accusations of scandal.

She employs two very different lenses for this analysis: that of a social scientist who examines the phenomenon as it occurs in communities and those whom it effects, and that of a theologian who evaluates the moral implications of the scandalous event as it unfolds and for those who learn of it later.

Angela touches every "hot-button issue" and point of tension in the last fifty years in the life of the church, but this work is not a partisan tirade or a diatribe. She approaches these very controversial issues with a balance that is objective, serious, and scholarly. Her hundreds of footnotes reveal both the extent of her labor and the quality of her sources.

As anomalous as it may seem, this book *Scandal* truly is a statement of hope: "One can expect that proclamation of God's reign will result in scandal just as it did when Jesus proclaimed it. This proclamation of God's reign led to the cross, but it did not end with the cross. The experience of God's love being stronger than sin and death provides a foundation for hope" (p. 99).

James A. Coriden
Washington Theological Union

Preface

Criminal and civil courts have held Catholic clergy accountable for sexual abuse of minors. The media have revealed failures by Catholic bishops and religious superiors to protect children and youth from such abuse. Catholic dioceses and religious provinces are filing for bankruptcy when they cannot bear the weight of the financial settlements. The desire to move beyond this scandal is real, and the steps taken have included responding to the needs of the survivors of sexual abuse and implementing policies and procedures to prevent future abuse. The complaint against Pope Benedict XVI that survivors of sexual abuse filed with the International Criminal Court in 2011 is a demand for more.

Were there never a case of sexual abuse, the Catholic Church would still be challenged to move beyond scandal in public life. Catholic colleges are accused of causing scandal when they invite certain commencement speakers. Catholic social service agencies are accused of scandal in light of concern about cooperation with laws compromising the institution's values. Catholic hospitals face the charge in relation to practices judged inconsistent with Catholic teaching about life, death, and sexuality. Catholics in political life have been denied Communion because their political positions are judged a source of scandal.

For the Catholic Church to faithfully engage in its mission of sharing God's love in the world, it needs to take time to reflect theologically on the ecclesial experience of scandal. Doing so will allow the Catholic Church to think critically about its tendency to focus on the principle of avoiding scandal in a narrow and absolute way. The practice of using the term "scandal" in relationship to emotionally charged issues makes avoiding theological reflection about scandal tempting.[1] This temptation, though, needs to be resisted so that concerns about scandal do not contribute to distortions in the community's life of faith and engagement in the world.

The Second Vatican Council plays a pivotal role in this theological reflection about scandal. Vatican II's call for the renewal of moral theology shifted theological reflection from a narrow focus on sin to a broader focus on the call to discipleship and in so doing led to less theological attention to scandal. At the same time, Vatican II's promotion of dialogue and collaboration in the world has increased the interactions that some in the church identify as scandalous. This ecclesial experience informed the adaptation of the traditional definition of scandal in the *Catechism of the Catholic Church*.[2]

Responding to Vatican II's call for theological reflection to be more biblical, our reflection will place emphasis on scandal as an obstacle to faith. Such a naming of scandal invites reflection on faith. Differences in the ways the First Vatican Council and the Second Vatican Council taught about faith and revelation are worth noting since this affects one's understanding of scandal defined in terms of faith. Differences in their understandings of church and its authority to teach also affect the appropriation of the term "scandal" in ecclesial discourse. Those emphasizing continuity between the councils display a tendency to retrieve Vatican I's teaching about faith, revelation, and church, and those emphasizing development tend to appeal to the teaching of Vatican II on faith, revelation, and church.

Both ecclesial change and social change have influenced the Catholic Church's engagement with the state and with society. With *Dignitatis Humanae* (Declaration on Religious Liberty), Catholic teaching changed from a call for state support for the Catholic Church to an appreciation of the religious liberty of all.[3] This fundamental human right to religious liberty receives great emphasis from Catholic leaders at the beginning of the second decade of the twenty-first century as both religious and secular states create laws that people experience as obstacles to faith. "Interpreting [the signs of the times] in the light of the Gospel" as called for by *Gaudium et Spes* (Pastoral Constitution on the Church in the Modern World), the church has been attentive to social movements, particularly as these have influenced the creation of new laws judged to be a source of scandal (GS 4).[4] In this changing environment, the Catholic identity of individuals and institutions receives greater attention, particularly as they are compromised through scandal in a sociological sense and are a source of scandal in the theological sense.

The introduction to this book provides a brief overview of scandal as a sign of the times. The first chapter examines the meaning of the term "scandal" from sociological, theological, and catechetical perspectives, noting similarities and differences in the use of the term. The case of clerical sexual abuse of minors illustrates both the sociological and the ecclesial meanings of the term. The second chapter examines the implications of different understandings of faith and revelation for interpreting scandal as an obstacle to faith. The third chapter focuses on the scandal of divisions within the church and within the life of the disciple. The fourth chapter considers the relationships among social movements, Catholic teaching, and scandal, as well as the criteria Catholics in public life use to identify scandal. The fifth chapter, attentive to the *Catechism*'s addition of laws and institutions as sources of scandal, examines the use of the language of scandal to evaluate individuals and institutions in public life.

Theological reflection about scandal and its effect on the church's mission in the world is essential if the church is to faithfully proclaim the Gospel. Lack of reflection risks truncating the tradition and obscuring the Good News. Church leadership continues to work to develop practical, concrete steps to avoid scandal in both a sociological and a theological

Acknowledgments

I am grateful to the many dialogue partners I have had as I have reflected on faith in public life through the years. Prominent among them have been Lisa Sowle Cahill, David Hollenbach, SJ, Michael Himes, Kenneth Himes, OFM, J. Bryan Hehir, Kevin Burke, SJ, and James Keenan, SJ. In addition to learning from these scholars, I have also learned from colleagues and students at the Washington Theological Union, as they have posed interesting questions and cases for consideration.

My research on the theological understanding of scandal has been enriched through scholarly presentations on scandal to the College Theology Society in 2003, to the New Wine, New Wineskins Conference for Catholic moral theologians at the University of Notre Dame in 2007, to Woodstock Theological Center at Georgetown University as a visiting fellow in 2007, and to the Catholic Theological Ethics in the World Church Conference in Trent, Italy, in 2010. My research into the political dimensions of the Catholic Church's international clerical sexual abuse scandal has benefited from the opportunity to be a research fellow at Georgetown University's Berkley Center for Religion, Peace, and World Affairs.

I am grateful for the financial support I have received for my research through a Vincent Cushing Research Grant from the Washington Theological Union, a summer research fellowship from the Wabash Center for Teaching and Learning in Theology and Religion, and a Lilly Theological Scholars Grant from the Association of Theological Schools. I appreciate the support of Georgetown University's Office of Scholarly and Literary Publications, directed by Carole Sargent, and the hospitality of the Georgetown Visitation Sisters. I thank Brian McDermott, SJ, for reading and offering perceptive observations about an earlier version of the manuscript. I am grateful to Peter Dwyer for inviting me to consider working with Liturgical Press on this project and to Hans Christoffersen and his colleagues for all they have done to make this book possible.

Introduction
Scandal as a Sign of the Times

As the Catholic bishops of the world concluded their meeting of the Second Vatican Council to update and renew the Catholic Church, they described a central activity of the church's mission: "reading the signs of the time and . . . interpreting them in the light of the Gospel" (*Gaudium et Spes* 4).[1] They saw a world in which there were movements for liberation—liberation from poverty, colonialism, patriarchy, and racism (see, e.g., GS 8–9). They also saw a world in which there were movements to liberalize laws regulating contraception, abortion, and divorce (see, e.g., GS 51, 47). They saw a world of diverse cultures (see, e.g., GS 53). They saw a world in need of greater political responsibility and peace (see e.g., GS 73, 77). They evaluated these signs of the times from the perspective of a Gospel that values human dignity and community (see, e.g., GS 12, 23–24). The Catholic faith community's engagement in the world, responding to these signs of the times, has divided its members for nearly a half century. Catholics differ in their evaluations of whether this activity promotes the Gospel or compromises the Gospel, resulting in scandal.

Forty-five years after *Gaudium et Spes* (Pastoral Constitution on the Church in the Modern World), Pope Benedict XVI drew particular attention to two signs of the times: violations of religious liberty and the scandal of sexual abuse of minors by clergy.[2] The need for greater religious liberty was not only a sign of the times at the end of the first decade of the twenty-first century; it was also a sign of the times to which the bishops of the Second Vatican Council dedicated an entire document in 1965.[3] In *Dignitatis Humanae* (Declaration on Religious Liberty), the bishops of the Second Vatican Council developed Catholic teaching from a position of state support, or at least religious liberty, for the Catholic Church to one of religious liberty for all (DH 1–8). In so doing, a teaching, thought to be infallible, changed. Benedict XVI has underscored the importance of this changed teaching as he has identified religious liberty as an aspect of "a sacred right to a full life" and as "at the origin of moral freedom."[4]

As Catholic individuals and institutions face new laws that require actions contrary to their values, they encounter the challenge of discerning a way to continue with integrity. Catholic leaders are noting that requiring Catholic institutions to act against their values is a violation of religious liberty.[5] To act against their values would result in scandal.[6]

Unlike religious liberty, clerical sexual abuse of minors was not an item on the agenda during the Second Vatican Council.[7] During the last two decades of the twentieth century, criminal and civil trials of priests accused of sexually abusing minors introduced the problem to the public and generated reflection among some bishops, particularly in the English-speaking world.[8] For these bishops, this was the moment to revise policies to more effectively protect the vulnerable from abuse; however, this was not true for all. For the latter and for many in the general public, denial was the response to such stories. These stories were short-lived in the media, as many people were not prepared to hear the accounts. In addition, when these accounts were heard, they were interpreted as exceptional cases. This perception was about to change.[9]

With the media's coverage of President Bill Clinton's sexual scandal, graphic description of sexual acts in the news became more commonplace.[10] With the development of the World Wide Web, more people have greater access to a story over an extended period of time. These are some of the circumstances that allowed the *Boston Globe*'s 2002 coverage of clerical sexual abuse of minors to have such national impact in the United States.[11] This coverage challenged earlier interpretations of abuse as exceptional cases; like the work of Jason Berry, it examined patterns of abuse and failures in church leadership to prevent these patterns.

In this same year, the Irish government established a commission to investigate the way in which ecclesial and civil authorities handled allegations of clerical sexual abuse of minors in the Archdiocese of Dublin.[12] Seven years later it released the Murphy Report.[13] This report from Ireland in 2009, as well as the Ryan Report that examined abuse in institutions (which were frequently run by religious), created the context in which the Jesuit president of Canisius College in Berlin proactively addressed his institution's history of sexual abuse of high school students, challenging assumptions that the problem was unique to the English-speaking world.[14] Country after country in Europe, as well as some from the Global South, reported such cases in 2010.[15] As the Catholic Church celebrated the year of the priest, Catholics became more aware of a hierarchical response that showed greater solidarity with accused priests than with victims of abuse.

The lack of solidarity with the victims compromised the church's mission of embodying and proclaiming the Good News of God's love for all, especially for the vulnerable. The failures of Catholic leaders to reflect God's preferential love for the vulnerable in this situation have undermined their ability to speak on behalf of the vulnerable in other situations and to respond to the material needs of the vulnerable.[16] Commenting on the situation in Ireland, the archbishop of Canterbury, Dr. Rowan Williams, observed: "An institution so deeply bound into the life of a society suddenly becoming, suddenly losing all credibility—that's not just a problem for the church, it is a problem for everybody in Ireland."[17] While the head of the Anglican communion was criticized for this comment, he rightly notes that the Catholic Church's credibility in public life was damaged by the clerical sexual abuse scandal, and this damage is certainly not limited to Ireland. As Catholics questioned the judgment and leadership of bishops, contributions to the special collections declined for dioceses in the United States, and the number of Germans paying the church tax declined in Germany.[18] This resulted in a decrease in diocesan funds to serve the poor through organizations like Catholic Charities. In addition, settlements and class action lawsuits have pushed some dioceses to the point of bankruptcy.[19] Because of actions that failed to protect children, not only were these young people hurt but so too were other vulnerable individuals.[20]

The contrast between actions that put more children at risk and advocacy for protection for the unborn has not been lost on observers. The Catholic Church's advocacy on behalf of the unborn is strong, and some bishops have told legislators who have voted to liberalize abortion laws that they would be denied Communion.[21] Catholic hospitals face the tension between generally accepted standards of care in obstetrics and gynecology, on the one hand, and the Catholic identity of the hospital, on the other, as seen in the case of a pregnant woman with pulmonary hypertension at St. Joseph Hospital in Phoenix, Arizona.[22] Not only have Catholic hospitals faced concerns about scandal associated with cooperation in evil but so too have Catholic social service agencies, due to changes in German abortion law and in US laws about health insurance, for instance.[23] Catholic schools face the charge of scandal when a commencement speaker's position on abortion is contrary to Catholic teaching. A high-profile example of this was the opposition to President Barack Obama as commencement speaker at the University of Notre Dame in 2009.[24]

Abortion and clerical sexual abuse are not the only issues leading to a judgment of scandal. In fact, a pro-life president who was the commencement speaker at the University of Notre Dame in 2006 faced the charge of scandal for other reasons. Protest of Ireland's President Mary McAleese as commencement speaker was based on her position in favor of women's ordination.[25] In 2010 the Cardinal Newman Society, continuing to monitor commencement speakers at Catholic colleges and universities, judged the presence of Bishop Kevin Dowling as commencement speaker at the University of San Francisco a scandal because he allows for the possibility of condoms being used to prevent the spread of HIV/AIDS.[26] Catholic health-care and social service agencies face similar judgments from others when their practices appear, or in fact are, contrary to Catholic teaching on such topics as contraception, homosexuality, marriage, and euthanasia.

Like the media, associations of Catholics are identifying scandals. They use the language of scandal found in both political life and ecclesial life. To better understand this language, we turn to a comparative analysis of the term "scandal" from sociological and ecclesial perspectives. This will inform our consideration of the Catholic Church's engagement in public life.

Talk about Scandal

CHAPTER 1

As Catholics talk about scandal, listen carefully to what is being said. At times they use the term in a generic way. At other times they use it in a specifically theological way. Catholics are identifying signs of the times as scandalous, and scandal is becoming a sign of the times.[1] Naming the clerical sexual abuse of minors a scandal is uncontested. In contrast, judgments about Catholic politicians' voting records and Catholic institutions' policies and practices as scandalous often both reflect and intensify divisions within the Catholic community.[2]

In this chapter, we will examine a sociological meaning of scandal in order to be able to analyze the use of the term in public life. We will also examine theological and catechetical understandings of scandal that have developed in the Catholic tradition. These multiple meanings inform Catholic discourse both in the faith community and in public life.

Scandal:
A Sociological Perspective

In order to better understand the term "scandal" in public discourse, we turn to a sociological perspective. Synthesizing an objectivist view of scandal that focuses on the wrongdoing and a constructivist view of scandal that focuses on the perception of the public, sociologist Ari Adut defines scandal as "an event of varying duration that starts with the publicization of a real, apparent, or alleged transgression to a negatively oriented audience and lasts as long as there is significant and sustained

public interest in it."[3] Analysis of scandal in light of this definition invites reflection on the act, the agent, the announcer,
and the audience. We will examine these elements operative in
scandal. Biblical stories will illustrate these elements. Because
of the reader's historical and cultural distance from the biblical text, these stories might provide illustrations that are less
likely than contemporary examples to distract from the analysis
of the term. After considering each element, we will evaluate
clerical sexual abuse in light of this understanding of scandal.

Act

The subject matter of a scandal from this sociological perspective could be an alleged wrongdoing, an apparent wrongdoing,
or an actual wrongdoing.[4] First, an accusation of wrongdoing,
whether true or false, can be sufficient subject matter for a
scandal. For example, Jesus was falsely accused of claiming
to be the King of the Jews, according to gospel accounts. In
response, Pilate questioned Jesus and did not find evidence to
substantiate the allegations, but he executed him nonetheless
to appease the Jewish leaders who brought the accusation
against him (see, e.g., Mark 15:1-15). Second, an action that
is not wrong but appears to people to be wrong can be sufficient subject matter for a scandal. When Jesus healed people
on the Sabbath, some were scandalized by his action. Some
interpreters of the law judged this to be work and therefore a
violation of the law prohibiting work on the Sabbath (see, e.g.,
Mark 3:1-6). In contrast, followers understood such action not
as work but as a reflection of the way in which God gives life
even on the Sabbath. Third, an action that is actually wrong
is the strongest foundation for a scandal. According to gospel
accounts, the apostle Peter denied knowing Jesus three times
after Jesus' arrest (see, e.g., Mark 14:66-72). In this, Peter was
not in right relationship with Jesus.

Some might question whether these examples actually pertain to wrongdoing. Wrongdoing from this sociological perspec-

tive could be a violation of social expectations, law, or morality.[5] If Jesus were to have claimed to be King of the Jews, such a claim would have violated social expectations. In the case of healing on the Sabbath, the apparent wrongdoing was that of violating the law. In the case of Peter denying Jesus, Peter was neither faithful nor honest and so acted contrary to morality. All three examples violate social expectations, and the latter two at least appear to violate the Jewish law. The categories are neither mutually exclusive nor identical.

Primarily, the word "wrongdoing" evaluates the morality of an action. Analogously, it describes violations of laws and social expectations. In contemporary discourse in Western secular societies, laws and social expectations often receive more attention than the morality of an act. Discussions about morality in pluralistic societies are often seen as violating the cultural value of tolerance by imposing one community's understanding of truth on another. A diversity of social expectations in the context of pluralism contributes to the possibility of one interpreting another's act as being contrary to social expectations. For the purposes of identifying scandal sociologically, an evaluation of the relationships among social expectations, law, and morality is not necessary. The violation of any one of the three is sufficient to identify an act as wrong, according to Adut's sociological perspective on scandal.[6] Not only is the act an important component of a scandal but so too is the agent.

Agent

The agent is the person who performs the wrongdoing. The role or status of this person contributes to the possibility of scandal.[7] When a person is in a position of power, there is an increased likelihood that others will be interested in the person's actions. People are typically more interested in the wrongdoing of a leader than of a follower.

The story of the Good Samaritan illustrates the significance of the agent's status. First, a priest fails to stop and help a man who had been beaten and robbed. He keeps his distance, walk-ing on the other side of the road. Then, a Levite does likewise. Finally, a Samaritan stops to help the injured man (Luke 10:25-37). The priest and Levite, religious leaders, neglected the needs of the injured man. In contrast, the Samaritan, who did not observe the law in the way that Jews expected, cared for the injured person. In this story, those of high religious status fail to respond to the injured person, whereas a person of low status did respond. As Jesus expands the audience's understanding of neighbor, he uses a contrast in status that draws attention to the observance of a religious purity law contributing to a failure to love a person in need.

With the assumption of leadership roles come greater respon-sibilities. People expect more from their leaders, whether these are religious leaders, political leaders, business leaders, military leaders, or cultural leaders. Because people are interested in the actions of these agents, they receive more attention. These agents are also susceptible to criticism for poor leadership when their subordinates engage in wrongdoing. Some try to cover up such wrongdoing in order to avoid scandal.[8]

Announcer

If no one knew about an agent's wrongdoing, there would be no scandal. From a sociological perspective, the wrongdoing (whether alleged, apparent, or actual) must be made public for scandal to occur.[9] The wrongdoing might be announced to an audience through the words, or even the act itself, of the agent. Often others (from the media to social network websites) play important roles in making the wrongdoing public.[10]

The ministry of Jesus can serve as an example of one's words and deeds announcing wrongdoing, insofar as his ministry in-cluded violations of social expectations and apparent violations of the law. Jesus announced the reign of God through word and deed. He invited people to repent and believe the Good News of God's saving love. He also revealed God's saving love through his acts of healing and forgiving sins. The act of forgiving sins was contrary to social expectations and considered contrary to the law since only God could forgive sins. This act of forgiving sins revealed the reign of God in the person of Jesus Christ, which challenged expectations.

A more indirect example of actions themselves making wrongdoing known occurs in a biblical account of the Hebrews enslaved in Egypt. According to the book of Exodus, the Hebrew midwives in Egypt acted contrary to the Pharaoh's command and did not kill the Hebrew male babies that they delivered. In the story, the birth of these children functions as an allegation that the midwives were violating the Pharaoh's command (Exod 1:15-22).

We find accounts not only of the words or actions of the agent announcing a wrongdoing but also of other people announcing the wrongdoing of the agent. The prophets announced that Israel was not faithful to its covenant with God. The people had worshipped idols instead of the one true God, and they needed to repent of this wrongdoing. The prophets named the community's violation of the law God had given, as well as God's desire for the people to return to the covenant.

The means for announcing an agent's wrongdoing have developed significantly since the time of the prophets. Contemporary technology allows a wrongdoing to be shared with a wider (even global) audience in a way that is unprecedented. Social media make the announcements accessible for a more extended (even indefinite) period of time. In order for the announcement of an agent's wrongdoing to become a scandal, there needs to be an interested audience.

Audience

Without an interested audience, there would be no scandal from a sociological perspective.[11] The interest reflects curiosity or emotional engagement with the event. The audience might experience embarrassment and shame or anger and outrage.

A negative orientation toward the event characterizes the interested audience.

In the Gospel of Matthew, concerns about a negatively interested audience first prevented Herod from killing John the Baptist and then propelled him to kill John the Baptist. The people admired John the Baptist as a prophet. One of his prophetic acts was telling King Herod that it was wrong for him to live with his brother's wife. Herod wanted to kill him; however, he only imprisoned him because he knew that the death of John the Baptist would be of interest to the people. Later, after delighting in his stepdaughter's dance, Herod promised to grant her whatever she requested. When her mother instructed her to ask for the head of John the Baptist, she did so before all those who were present. King Herod knew that if he went back on his word to grant her request, those present would form an interested audience that would negatively evaluate as a wrongdoing this betrayal of his promise (Matt 14:1-12).

In times of political, economic, and cultural instability, when people are fearful and more negatively inclined, an interested audience with a negative orientation is not hard to find. In the midst of cultural divisions, audience interpretations of wrongdoing often vary. At times, subgroups judge the agent's wrongdoing negatively for different reasons. With this as background, we turn to an uncontested case of sociological scandal during the first decade of the twenty-first century: the sexual abuse of minors by Catholic clergy.

Clerical Sexual Abuse of Minors as Sociological Scandal

To evaluate the phenomenon of ecclesial scandal from a sociological perspective, we now consider the public's response to clerical sexual abuse of minors. We will look for all four elements described above: act, agent, announcer, and audience. In the three countries mentioned in the introduction (the United States, Ireland, and Germany), sexually abusing minors is an act that is contrary to social expectations and laws as well as to morality. Knowledge of such wrongdoing generates outrage. As people read allegations, the assumption that they are true is sufficient to generate a reaction to such wrongdoing.[12]

In cases of clerical sexual abuse, the agents are in positions of trust. There is a common expectation within both church and society that those who preach to others about how to live will embody the message that they preach. The common sociological dynamic of associating one agent's wrongdoing with individuals at a higher level in an organization occurred as stories of sexual abuse by clergy moved to stories of bishops, and even the pope, failing to prevent further abuse.

The cases were announced to the public through the actions of the state, through the media, through grassroots organizations, and even at times by ecclesial leaders. In some countries, civil and criminal court cases revealed wrongdoing by priests and their superiors, which the media reported. In others, government-appointed commissions gathered information to share with the public. Grassroots organizations like Survivors Network of those Abused by Priests have empowered individuals to share their stories with the public. When accused of sexually abusing a seminarian, Cardinal Joseph Bernardin held a press conference to make the accusation public and announce that diocesan protocols for investigating accusations would be followed.

By the twenty-first century, there was an interested public that was ready to hear the story not only of the actions of particular priests but also of the leadership of the hierarchy. The audience's negative orientation toward the hierarchy is attributable to more than one cause. Among those causes are conflicting values on particular moral issues and between clerical culture and liberal culture itself. A divided Catholic Church could unite in opposition to the wrongdoing of clerical sexual abuse of minors and to failures in leadership to prevent it, even if individuals differed in interpretations of the causes and in judgments about necessary action steps.[13]

Sociological scandal reflects a failure in public relations. Papal and episcopal concern about public relations is often expressed in terms of protecting the reputation of the church, as seen in the National Review Board report from the United States and the Murphy Report from Ireland.[14] These reports indicate that bishops were concerned about both the reputation of the church and scandal. In these reports, the reputation of the church and scandal are not synonymous. In light of this, we will turn to Catholic theological and catechetical perspectives on scandal.

Scandal: Catholic Theological and Catechetical Perspectives

Contemporary Catholic discourse about scandal is deeply indebted to the thirteenth-century Dominican theologian Thomas Aquinas. He wrote the *Summa Theologica* to prepare people for ministry.[15] In the wake of the Fourth Lateran Council, which called for annual confession, preparation of confessors was particularly important.[16] Three centuries later, this was no less true. After the Protestant Reformation called both the practice of confession and the qualifications of the clergy into question, the Council of Trent called for seminaries in each diocese and was attentive to the formation of confessors.[17] In these seminaries, moral theology developed as a distinct discipline. As the purpose of the discipline of moral theology was to prepare confessors, the theology of Thomas Aquinas served as the foundation of the curriculum. As a result, Catholic theological reflections on scandal have generally been based on, or at least have been in conversation with, the theology of Aquinas. To better understand ecclesial discourse about scandal, we now turn to Aquinas's understanding of scandal.

Aquinas on Scandal

Aquinas begins with a biblical understanding of scandal from the tradition.[18] The Greek word σκάνδαλον (*skandalon*) found in the New Testament refers to a stumbling block. To interpret the use of this word in Scripture, Aquinas turns to the writing of Jerome, the patristic translator of and commentator on Scripture. Jerome explains the meaning of the term as he comments on Matthew 15:12. In this passage the Pharisees are scandalized when Jesus says that nothing that enters the mouth defiles a person. The Pharisees emphasized the importance of observance of the law for one's relationship with God, and the Jewish law prohibited the consumption of unclean food. Hearing Jesus' statement that nothing that one eats defiles a person challenged their faith. Jerome interprets the literal meaning of scandal in the context of Matthew 18:6, in which Jesus instructs his disciples not to lead a child to sin. Based on this, Jerome understands "Whoever 'scandalizes' any of the least of these" to mean "the one who by word or deed gives to anyone an occasion for falling."[19] This serves as the foundation for Aquinas's definition of scandal: "something less rightly done or said, that occasions another's spiritual downfall."[20] Aquinas's addition of "less rightly done" to the definition qualifies the words or deeds under consideration. As he reflects on his addition, he turns to Paul's instructions to the Corinthians and the Romans to be attentive that they not appear to engage in idolatry through their consumption of food and thus influence another to sin (1 Cor 8:10; Rom 14:21).[21] In this way, Aquinas notes that not only could one's wrong actions tempt another to sin but so too could actions that appear wrong.

Aquinas's reflection on scandal is enriched by a number of sources. After adopting the definition of Jerome, he incorporates further biblical reflection. He turns in particular to the Gospel of Matthew and the letters of Paul, which are the scriptural texts that most often use the term σκάνδαλον (*skandalon*). Jerome is not the only Doctor of the Church whom Aquinas cites; he also engages the writing of Augustine and Gregory the Great.[22] In addition, just as Augustine's theology engaged neoplatonist philosophy, Aquinas's engages the philosophy of Aristotle.

Aquinas uses technical philosophical terms such as "direct" and "accidental" to evaluate the intention of the person creating an obstacle for another.[23] Direct scandal is an act in which the agent intends to tempt another to sin. In contrast, accidental scandal refers to wrong or apparently wrong actions that could unintentionally influence another to sin. Intending to tempt another to sin is a sin that is directly contrary to charity, the virtue oriented toward friendship with God.[24]

Scandal is a relational reality that involves two individuals exercising their freedom. Often there is a person creating an obstacle through an action, and there is a person responding to an obstacle.[25] A person might exercise freedom in a number of ways that could result in an obstacle from a morally wrong action. First, a person could act in a way that is wrong in order to tempt another to sin. Second, a person could act in a way that is wrong and in which one foresees but does not intend to create an obstacle. Third, a person could act in a way that is wrong but not consider the effect of one's action on another. In all of these situations, Aquinas notes that sinful activity creates the obstacle. He describes all of these situations as active scandal because an agent is creating an obstacle that could tempt a person to sin. While all of these cases are active scandal, only the first is also direct scandal. Only in the case of direct active scandal is the obstacle intended. While Aquinas describes all of these forms of active scandal as sinful because of the sinful act of the agent, in the case of direct active scandal, as we have noted, the intention to influence another to sin is also a specific sin contrary to the virtue of charity.[26]

Aquinas does not limit the obstacles to *wrong* actions. In fact, it could appear that anything that is not perfect is a scandal. This, however, is not what his addition of "less rightly done" to Jerome's definition of scandal means. Instead, he recognizes that actions appearing wrong are obstacles that could tempt another to stumble.[27] As noted above, the Corinthians who ate meat sacrificed to idols might appear to participate in idolatry even if they believed in and worshipped the one true God (see also 1 Cor 10:23-33). Others might find their action an obstacle regardless of whether those who ate the meat affected their relationship with God by doing so.

The obstacle is an occasion for sin, according to Aquinas. The obstacle does not cause another person to sin.[28] The other person remains free to choose how to respond to the obstacle. The obstacle makes a sinful response more likely, but the person responding remains free not to sin. In other words, a person strong in faith will not succumb to the obstacle created by another.[29] In such a case, if the obstacle were intended to occasion the sin of another, the one who acted against charity through direct active scandal would have sinned, but the one who resisted the temptation would not have sinned.

Interactions between Jesus and the Pharisees might suggest that good actions can also be obstacles; however, in such a case, the obstacle that occasions their sin is the malice within them. Malice is not the only potential obstacle within the one who takes scandal; ignorance is another.[30] Aquinas identifies these types of scandal as passive scandal. Aquinas calls for educating the ignorant, if circumstances permit, so as to avoid this type of scandal. He is clear that truth should not be sacrificed in an effort to avoid scandal of the weak. In similar fashion, the malice of others is not to deter one in pursuing the good. In this case, the one performing the good act does not bear responsibility for the scandal if another sins in response to this good act. Stories of Pharisees taking scandal at Jesus' proclamation of God's reign provide a good example to Christ's followers to continue responding faithfully to God even when others respond destructively to this.

To review, Aquinas's writing on scandal is faithful to the biblical term σκάνδαλον (*skandalon*). He is attentive to the term's literal meaning: an obstacle that could cause another to stumble.[31] While Scripture and Jerome's commentary on Scripture are Aquinas's primary sources, the analysis is philosophical, as he distinguishes first between active and passive scandal and then between direct and accidental active scandal, as well as between passive scandal due to weakness and passive scandal due to malice. These distinctions allow him to analyze the sin of scandal in terms of matter and gravity and to consider the circumstances in which one has an obligation to forego a good so as not to scandalize a neighbor.[32] In the context of his consideration of the theological virtue of charity, he identifies scandal as a vice contrary to beneficence and defines it as "something less rightly done or said, that occasions another's spiritual downfall."[33]

Moral Theology from Trent to Vatican II on Scandal

Aquinas defined the terms in which moral theology has evaluated scandal. Whether one looks to Francisco Suarez, SJ, of sixteenth-century Spain, Alphonsus Liguori, CSsR, of eighteenth-century Naples, Bishop Francis Kenrick of nineteenth-century America, Henry Davis, SJ, of twentieth-century England, or Fritz Tillmann and Bernard Häring, CSsR, of twentieth-century Germany, each was indebted to the work of Aquinas. This was surely to be expected from Suarez, who offers a commentary on Aquinas's *Summa Theologica*.[34] Alphonsus Liguori incorporates cases, and the opinions of respected moral theologians regarding those cases, into a Thomistic analysis of scandal.[35] The seminary manuals of moral theology from that of Kenrick in the latter half of the nineteenth century to that of Davis in the early twentieth century rely heavily on the work of both Alphonsus Liguori, the patron saint of moral theologians, and Thomas Aquinas.[36] This is most obvious in Kenrick's writing, which quotes Alphonsus Liguori and Thomas Aquinas with noticeable frequency, just as Aquinas's writing on scandal quotes Scripture and Jerome. This writing about the sin of scandal prepared a confessor to evaluate the sin in terms of intention, circumstances, and gravity in concrete cases. The cases and philosophical distinctions were to help confessors as they judged a penitent's sinful actions.

Bringing the biblical renewal into moral theology, Tillmann and Häring situate their discussion of scandal under the second great commandment, rather than the theological virtue of charity, in *The Master Calls* and *The Law of Christ*.[37] The former Scripture scholar and the Redemptorist, who had desired to be a Scripture scholar, present moral theology in biblical and christocentric terms. Writing handbooks of moral theology intentionally for the laity, rather than exclusively for the seminarian, they emphasize the Christian's call to holiness, in contrast with the manualists.[38] These developments, later affirmed by the bishops of the Second Vatican Council as they called for the renewal of moral theology, signaled the beginning of a shift in theological reflection, including that on scandal.[39]

In *The Law of Christ*, Häring analyzes the term "scandal" in the general and biblical senses. This leads to a sustained reflection on Jesus Christ as scandal. Following the lead of the New Testament use of σκάνδαλον (*skandalon*), Häring recognizes that expressions both of God's love and of human sinfulness can function as obstacles that cause another to stumble. In this reflection on scandal, Häring describes the sin of mediocrity in the church. This writing laid the groundwork for *Gaudium et Spes* (Pastoral Constitution on the Church in the Modern World) identifying the scandal of discontinuity between faith and life.[40] As Häring ends his discussion of scandal, he returns to common cases from the tradition pertaining to sexuality, yet he also states that "it would be a fatal error to overlook the risk of scandal possible in other areas such as industry and social relations."[41] In this, he foreshadows the concern about institutions and laws as sources of scandal that developed after the Second Vatican Council and is reflected in the *Catechism of the Catholic Church*, published three decades after the council.[42]

This *Catechism of the Catholic Church* adapts the traditional theological understanding of scandal in significant ways. The purpose of the *Catechism* is to form and inform Catholics' understanding of their faith. Theological reflection on the *Catechism*'s teaching about scandal has been lacking. In light of this, we will reflect on this teaching first in relationship to past councils and then in relationship to the *Summa Theologica*.

Councils and Catechisms on Scandal:
Comparing Trent and Vatican II

Concern about scandalous ecclesial practices in the sixteenth century had inspired Erasmus and Martin Luther alike to work for reform, albeit in different ways. When the bishops gathered in Trent, they too wrote about reform that needed to be implemented. They did not tend to use the language of scandal in their writing at the council, and the *Roman Catechism* produced after the Council of Trent did not reflect on scandal. In contrast, four centuries later at the Second Vatican Council, the spirit of *ressourcement* invited use of the biblical language of scandal. The bishops used this language to name divisions: within the body of Christ calling for ecumenism,[43] within the life of the disciple calling for more faithful evangelical witness (GS 43), and within the human family calling for the promotion of the dignity of the human person (GS 29, 88).

Three decades after the Second Vatican Council, the Vatican issued a catechism. This catechism includes a reflection on scandal informed by four significant experiences of the church in the intervening years. First, in response to the conclusions against the use of artificial contraception in Paul VI's 1968 encyclical *Humanae Vitae* (On the Regulation of Birth), a significant number of Catholics dissented, and some did so publicly.[44] The Vatican spoke critically of this as an attitude of dissent. Second, laws regarding contraception, abortion, divorce, homosexuality, and euthanasia were changing in some countries during this period to allow practices contrary to Catholic teaching about human flourishing. Catholic participation in political life at times supported these changes. Third, these legal changes at times had implications for the policies and practices of Catholic institutions, particularly those specializing in the areas of health care, social services, and education. Fourth, during this time cases of clerical sexual abuse of minors received attention from members of the hierarchy. All of these events inform the consideration of scandal in the *Catechism of the Catholic Church*.

Comparing the Catechism *and the* Summa *on Scandal*

According to the *Catechism*, "Scandal is an attitude or behavior which leads another to do evil. The person who gives scandal becomes his neighbor's tempter."[45] This initial statement about scandal changes the traditional language of "word or deed" in the definition to "attitude or behavior."[46] In addition, it focuses on the one who gives scandal without much attention to the one who takes scandal.

To better understand this new language of "attitude or behavior" as the obstacle, one needs to recall the promulgation of *Humanae Vitae*. Paul VI had not allowed the Second Vatican Council to teach about contraception. The results of a papal commission on birth control, recommending that Catholic teaching allow for married couples to use contraceptives for the purpose of responsible parenthood, had been leaked to the press. Catholics expected a change in teaching about the use of contraceptives in marriage, but that did not happen. Dissent from *Humanae Vitae* was not simply discussed in scholarly theological journals but also expressed publicly through the media. The Vatican described this opposition to the teaching as an attitude of dissent in the church. The negative orientation of many toward the conclusions of *Humanae Vitae* was a formative experience after Vatican II and drew attention to the role of attitudes in tempting others.

Note the way in which aspects of the sociological understanding of scandal have influenced the adaptation of the theological understanding in this catechism. The church experienced the media making known the dissatisfaction of prominent Catholics with the teaching of *Humanae Vitae*. Others, who were already negatively inclined in response to the conclusions of the teaching, were interested in the media's coverage. The conditions were present for sociological scandal as a result of this teaching. Teaching was not the only act that generated sociological scandal in this case. Acts of public dissent from the teaching also resulted in sociological scandal, as others were negatively oriented toward this behavior. In this context, an expression of dissatisfaction with a teaching leads another to a response of dissatisfaction toward a person who expresses dissatisfaction with a teaching. This is the dynamic so frequently operative in commencement controversies, and the controversies indicate that the dynamic is not limited to teaching about the use of contraceptives.

According to the *Catechism*'s presentation, even if there is no behavior that communicates one's attitude, the attitude alone could tempt another. This raises the question of how one would know the attitude. This question of knowing is precisely the reason Aquinas chose to use the language of words and deeds in his discussion of scandal.[47] He chose not to include desires or thoughts in his definition. He recognized that even those that are sinful, if they are not expressed, do not influence another to sin.

Aquinas's approach of focusing on a particular, observable act also challenges the contemporary tendency to move to character judgments based on one's perception of another's attitude toward a teaching. He showed epistemological humility, which is important since the human being, created in God's image, is mystery. Not only is the fact of the other being mystery important but so too are the limitations of one's ability to perceive accurately. One's own fears and emotions can affect one's perception and interpretation of another's attitude. This is not an uncommon phenomenon for a church in the midst of change.

The *Catechism*'s presentation of scandal is also less attentive to freedom. Aquinas consciously chooses to use "occasions" another's sin, rather than "causes" another's sin, in order to maintain the freedom of the one who takes scandal. In fact, Aquinas reflects explicitly on the freedom of the one who might stumble. He recognizes that even if one person acts deliberately to lead another to sin, that other person might freely choose not to sin. Conversely, a person might act in a way that is good, and another, due to either ignorance or malice, might respond sinfully. In the case of ignorance, love of neighbor calls for educating the ignorant, if possible, before doing good, in order to avoid scandal. In the case of malice, the malice of another should not inhibit one from doing good, as stories of Jesus responding to Pharisees suggest.

Situating the discussion of scandal under the fifth commandment and using the heading of "Respect for the Souls of Others: Scandal," the *Catechism* considers only the agency of the one who might lead another to sin. The *Catechism* recognizes that the weakness of the other intensifies scandal, but it does not consider the way in which one might address this through education, as Aquinas suggested. In contrast with Aquinas, a consideration of the potential malice of the one scandalized is missing in the *Catechism*'s presentation of scandal. In fact, the reflection on using power in such a way that it leads another to sin does not take into account that the power might be exercised for good and that the malice of the other might cause scandal in response to the good done.[48] In this way, the *Catechism* holds one responsible for the evil another does out of malice in response to a good action.

Another part of the *Catechism* focused on the person of Jesus Christ states, "Jesus scandalized the Pharisees by eating with tax collectors and sinners. . . . Jesus gave scandal above all when he identified his merciful conduct toward sinners with God's own attitude toward them."[49] In this section on "Jesus and Israel's Faith in the One God and Savior," the *Catechism* also explains that " 'ignorance' and the 'hardness' of their unbelief" led the Sanhedrin to call for Jesus' death.[50] This, however, is not integrated into its reflection on scandal.

Aquinas's more nuanced consideration of scandal allows for an integration of all of this, whereas the *Catechism*'s description of scandal would leave Jesus responsible for leading the Pharisees and Sanhedrin into evil as a result of his proclamation of the reign of God, even though that is not the *Catechism*'s conclusion in the christological section. Contextualizing scandal in terms of lack of respect for the soul of another, the *Catechism* narrows its reflection on scandal. This reflection on scandal does not consider the freedom and agency of the other, as Aquinas's does.

Aquinas describes scandal in theological terms, whereas the *Catechism* tends to use moral terms with greater frequency. Aquinas focuses on acts that could lead to another's spiritual downfall (mortal sin) or stumbling (venial sin). He evaluates the mortal, venial, or apparent sin of the one who gives scandal and the mortal or venial sin of the one who takes scandal. He identifies a special sin against the virtue of charity in cases where one intends to lead another to sin. In contrast with Aquinas's use of the language of sin, the *Catechism* rarely uses the language of sin in its discussion of scandal; instead, it uses the moral language of leading another to do evil. The *Catechism* first describes the result of scandal as damage to virtue and integrity, and it only later identifies a result in spiritual terms as it recognizes the possibility of spiritual death (mortal sin). It returns quickly to the language of morality as it talks about grave offenses. The *Catechism* states that this offense could be either a deed or an omission. This is a reminder that it is not only the evil that one does but also the good that one fails to do that negatively affects others.[51] In another context, the *Catechism* illustrates such an omission as it describes a lack of response to famine as a scandalous injustice.[52]

Both Aquinas and the *Catechism* recognize that authority contributes to the seriousness of scandal. The *Catechism* provides a more developed and explicit reflection on authority and scandal. For instance, it considers the authority of one with a responsibility to teach. In so doing, the *Catechism*'s language of nature and office is rather abstract.[53] Interpreted in light of other magisterial documents, it includes not only parents and teachers but also bishops and theologians. In fact, if one takes *Lumen Gentium* (Dogmatic Constitution on the Church) seriously, it includes all of the baptized in light of their responsibility to share in the prophetic office of Christ (LG 31).

The *Catechism* does not limit its consideration of authority to teachers but rather provides a general list of others. Based on its identification of laws, institutions, fashions, and opinions as obstacles, it names some who are responsible for them:

lawmakers, business leaders, and shapers of public opinion.[54] This is not to be found in Aquinas's reflection on scandal. Later, Alphonsus Liguori and his contemporaries evaluated cases involving fashion and opinion; however, the interpersonal focus of the confessional did not draw attention to laws and institutions as sources of scandal. An orientation toward dialogue and collaboration after Vatican II and an environment marked by social movements advocating change, including change that conflicted with Catholic teaching about life and human flourishing, created the conditions for identifying new laws as a source of scandal. These same conditions contributed to conversations about ecclesial identity in Catholic education, health care, and social service agencies and raised awareness about institutions as a source of scandal. With this attentiveness to institutions as a source of scandal, we turn to a consideration of clerical sexual abuse as scandal from a theological perspective.

Clerical Sexual Abuse of Minors as Theological Scandal

In January 2002, the *Boston Globe* began to run a series of articles drawing attention to the problem of child sexual abuse by clergy in the Archdiocese of Boston.[55] The stories appeared as former priest John Geoghan was being tried for child sexual abuse. At one level, these stories draw attention to the abusive behavior of individual priests toward children and youth. This foundational layer of individual scandal illustrates the traditional theological definition of scandal. At another level, these stories provide evidence that institutional attempts to avoid scandal became a source of scandal. This case provides an opportunity to examine the definition from Aquinas and note recent adaptations in the *Catechism*.

At the foundational layer of individual scandal, whether others take scandal or not, this abusive behavior is an occasion that could lead to another's spiritual harm. The testimony of both those who were abused and other Catholics points to the spiritual harm experienced from this abusive behavior. Taking into account the evil of the action, the authority of the priest, and the vulnerability of the young, John Paul II stated: "Like you, I too have been deeply grieved by the fact that priests and religious, whose vocation it is to help people live holy lives in the sight of God, have themselves caused such suffering and scandal to the young."[56] This statement to the US cardinals, echoing the *Catechism of the Catholic Church*, acknowledges the way in which authority associated with the priesthood intensified the scandalous behavior of these individuals.

Because of the way church leadership responded to a significant number of cases of clerical sexual abuse, the source of scandal was not limited to individuals. Institutional scandal resulted from the practices of concealing abusive behavior and of assigning these priests to new parishes. These actions have occasioned responses that do not embody love of God and neighbor. In a letter to priests, Cardinal Bernard Law acknowledged the detrimental effect of making decisions based on the desire to avoid scandal.[57] The Archdiocese of Boston is just one instance in which attempts to avoid scandal functioned as a source of scandal. Efforts to avoid scandal of the weak became an occasion for scandal. The case of clerical sexual abuse illustrates both individuals and institutions as sources of scandal in the theological sense.

The *Catechism* and Clerical Sexual Abuse of Minors

Since church leaders involved in the drafting of the *Catechism*, such as Cardinal Bernard Law and then-Cardinal Joseph Ratzinger, knew about cases of clerical sexual abuse in the years prior to the publication of the *Catechism*, one might ask to what degree the *Catechism* was influenced by this. For instance, the following judgment appears to reflect listening to the voices of victims: "Connected to incest is any sexual abuse perpetrated by adults on children or adolescents entrusted to their care. The offense is compounded by the scandalous harm done to the physical and moral integrity of the young, who will remain scarred by it all their lives; and the violation of responsibility for their upbringing."[58] Such a judgment calls for solidarity with those who have experienced this abuse.[59]

Given this judgment, one might ask why that solidarity was not demonstrated earlier and more comprehensively and why actions were not taken to inform parishes or governments about the abuse so as to prevent further abuse. The *Catechism*'s evaluation of the relationship between scandal and truth sheds light on this. A section titled "Respect for the Truth," which actually emphasizes withholding the truth, states, "The duty to avoid scandal often commands strict discretion. No one is bound to reveal the truth to someone who does not have the right to know it."[60] This raises the question of who has a right to know. In this case, one could certainly point to the *Catechism*'s acknowledgment that professional secrets should not be kept when they could result in great harm.[61] This would challenge the course of action too frequently taken. In addition, the *Catechism* acknowledges the need for balance between the common good and individual rights, and one could certainly point to failures to protect the common good in these situations of abuse that focused on the individual rights of priests.[62] Often ecclesial leaders appear to have concluded that neither the parish nor the state had a right to know this information in order to prevent harm and protect the common good.

Aquinas offers a contrasting perspective on the relationship between truth and scandal. Aquinas quotes Gregory the Great, who states, "If people are scandalized at the truth, it is better to allow the birth of scandal, than to abandon the truth."[63] Aquinas would oppose the use of the principle of avoiding scandal when it results in the sacrifice of the truth. Aquinas advocates avoiding scandal of the weak more through education than through secrecy.

From Conversation Stopper
to Conversation Starter

Whether responding with silence or outrage, Catholics have difficulty talking about the clerical sexual abuse scandal. The association of clerical sexual abuse and scandal is enough for many to equate the two terms when thinking about the life of the Catholic Church. This tragic, uncontested case of sociological and theological scandal often limits critical thinking about the language of scandal.

Some Catholics use the language of scandal to communicate judgment against Catholic institutions and individuals. This use of the term in public life is narrower than in the theological tradition and often reflects divisions in the Catholic Church over the appropriation of the Second Vatican Council. Such use of the language of scandal invites theological reflection on underlying differences in views about faith, church, and engagement in the world. With this in mind, we will follow the council's call for theological reflection to be more biblical and turn to a theological reflection on scandal as an obstacle to faith.

Scandal:
Stumbling Block to Faith

CHAPTER 2

The biblical understanding of scandal as a stumbling block to faith invites reflection on the meaning of faith.[1] Contemporary Catholics have different operative understandings of faith, depending on whether they emphasize continuity with the First Vatican Council or development with the Second Vatican Council. This affects their understanding of the meaning of scandal as an obstacle to faith.

In this chapter we will begin with an overview of faith from systematic and historical perspectives. To better understand the use of the term "faith" within the Catholic community, we will compare the ways in which the First Vatican Council and the Second Vatican Council taught about faith and revelation. Then, we will consider obstacles to faith that receive little attention in Catholic ethicists' reflections on scandal. First, we will reflect on language and ideas about God as obstacles to faith and then on persecution and laws limiting religious liberty as obstacles to faith.

Faith: A Catholic Perspective

The Catholic tradition has talked about faith in terms of *fides qua* (act of faith) and *fides quae* (content of faith). Some Catholics are tempted to focus on the content of faith to the neglect of their relationship with God. Other Catholics are tempted to focus on faith in God without attending to the content of faith that the Christian community professes. In contrast, we will maintain the classic "both/and" approach regarding *fides qua* and *fides quae* as we consider faith from systematic and historical perspectives.

Faith: Responding to Mystery in History

Faith is a response of trust in God who is Mystery. This Mystery did not choose to remain hidden, but rather God has communicated God's self to us, as Karl Rahner explains.[2] Faith is one's trusting response to this revelation of God. In the primary instance, faith is a response to the encounter with "mystery that grounds and supports all that is."[3]

These encounters with Mystery have taken place within history, and the community of believers remembers formative encounters from this history. The most formative encounter for the Christian community is God's self-revelation in the life, death, and resurrection of Jesus Christ. Christian faith is not simply knowledge about God's past actions in history but a relationship with a God who continues to act in the lives of individuals and communities. This faith is both personal (as opposed to abstract) and communal (as opposed to private). Human beings are social by nature and learn to name experiences of God in terms of the language of their communities. For Christians, this naming cannot be done apart from community. As a historical religion, Christianity cannot be known apart from members of the community sharing God's revelation in the person of Jesus Christ. This happens through both word (written or oral) and witness.

Professing and Living the Faith

From Mary Magdalene and John to Peter and Paul, the apostles experienced the revelation of God in the person of Jesus Christ.[4] The revelation of God's reign was made manifest in the teaching and healing ministry of Jesus. Mary, John, and

Peter were among the eyewitnesses who informed the faith of later apostles like Paul. Through Jesus' life, death, and resurrection, they all came to know more fully the God of Abraham and Sarah, Isaac and Rebekah, Jacob and Rachel. They came to know more fully the God who creates, sustains, and liberates.

From Paul's early correspondence with Christian communities that he founded to the gospel accounts that communities proclaimed and later recorded, one sees written expressions of the community's experience of God's revelation. Christians have understood God's revelation in the person of Jesus Christ to be the fulfillment of God's saving activity in Israel's history. They have relied on the Holy Spirit to guide the community in recognizing those accounts that faithfully communicate that revelation.[5]

Through the person of Jesus Christ, God revealed who God is for them, and their response was faith. This happened in the context of community, and the community gave expression to this experience of Jesus Christ as Lord. This profound experience reoriented their lives, and they wanted to share the Good News they experienced with others.

As people prepared to enter the community of faith, to become part of the Body of Christ, they discovered that professing faith in Jesus Christ as Lord called for giving witness to this new relationship in every aspect of their lives. Through the community, they were invited to know God, who is Mystery, in a new way. The community shared its experience of God as Creator, Redeemer, and Sanctifier. It shared its understanding of the Good News of God's reign, which called for a response. An early example of how this Christian response of faith was shared with catechumens can be found in the *Didache*.[6] This taught catechumens about the way of life that Christians followed—a way of life grounded in love of God and neighbor and in prayer and thanksgiving.

At baptism, catechumens would profess the faith of the community as an expression of their own faith. Christians were united in their acceptance of God's revelation kept alive in the community by the power of the Holy Spirit. They professed their faith in one God: Father, Son, and Spirit.

As Christians engaged one another and the larger Greco-Roman world in which they lived, they needed to be able to give an account of their hope (1 Pet 3:15). Professions of faith like the Apostles' Creed gave voice to the community's faith but did not explain it.[7] As Christians sought to better understand and explain their faith, diverse theologies developed. At times, these diverse theologies would be incompatible and raise the question of what the community truly believed. In such situations, the bishops, as the center of unity in their respective local churches, would gather together to resolve the conflict in the community's expression of faith.[8]

In the fourth century the emperor Constantine called for such a council. This first ecumenical council called by Constantine gathered in Nicaea and responded to the division within the community about the divinity of Christ. It determined that Arius's view against Christ's divinity was not the faith of the community.[9] The more developed creed that it issued reflects this judgment about the faith.[10] This creed is the core of the liturgical profession of faith for many Christian denominations in the East and the West. Since the first ecumenical council, councils have taught about the content of faith. At the two most recent worldwide councils of Catholic bishops, cultural challenges to belief have invited reflection not only on faith but also on revelation.

From Vatican I to Vatican II: Teaching about Faith and Revelation

By the late nineteenth century, the Catholic bishops of the world began to address modern challenges to belief with explicit teaching about revelation and faith.[11] The First Vatican Council met six years after Pope Pius IX issued the Syllabus of Errors and taught about faith in terms of both the category of error and the content of those errors.[12] In addition, the reception of the teaching of the Council of Trent, which responded to the Protestant Reformation, shaped its reflection. In fact, the First Vatican Council began with the Tridentine profession of faith. This profession of faith contained not only the teaching of the Nicene-Constantinopolitan Creed with the inclusion of the *filioque*[13] but also the affirmation of Catholic teaching and practices that were challenged during the Protestant Reformation, including the role of the Catholic Church in the interpretation of Scripture and the role of traditions in the life of the faith community.[14]

The First Vatican Council's *Dei Filius* (Dogmatic Constitution on the Catholic Faith) identified concerns resulting from the Protestant Reformation and the Enlightenment. In relationship to the former, the bishops highlighted rejection of the magisterium for the sake of independent judgments, resulting in both divisions and loss of faith in Christ. In relationship to the latter, they reiterated concerns found in the Syllabus of Errors about rationalism, naturalism, and pantheism. With an understanding of reason and faith as mutually informing, they responded to the inadequacies in the presupposition that reasoned arguments will yield faith, on the one hand, and in descriptions of faith as blind or as a leap, on the other. With regard to nature, they offered a critique of pantheism, the identification of Creator and creation, on the one hand, and of an atheistic materialism in which the material world exists without a Creator, on the other. The First Vatican Council was also concerned about confusion among Catholics regarding the relationship of nature and grace as well as the relationship of human knowledge and divine faith. With these concerns in mind, the bishops of the First Vatican Council taught about God, revelation, faith, and reason. This teaching was a response to challenges posed by Enlightenment understandings of reason and its relationship to revelation and faith.[15]

This teaching about Catholic faith reflected not on the whole Creed but rather on the first article: the belief in God the Creator.[16] Engaging philosophical reason, the bishops presented divine attributes of God, reflecting an understanding of God as accessible to all since the Creator can be known through reasoned reflection on creation. This was a response to those who would consider belief in God unreasonable. The bishops were clear that natural revelation is not all that there is to say; there is more beyond this. They described this "more" as supernatural revelation, which includes both the written word and unwritten tradition that the apostles received from Christ and handed down with the assistance of the Holy Spirit. The bishops affirmed the canon of Scripture from Trent as sacred and canonical, written under inspiration.[17] As they turned from revelation to faith, they identified faith as a gift and as a supernatural virtue. They described this gift in terms of belief: with it, one "believe[s] to be true what [God] has revealed."[18] *Dei Filius* presented faith in terms of the content of faith, *fides quae*.

In the decades following Vatican I, Catholic Scripture scholars and Catholic theologians engaged their contemporary situation with its attentiveness to history. As Catholic Scripture scholars took history seriously, they used new methods to interpret Scripture. As Catholic theologians of *nouvelle théologie* considered the community's understanding of revelation, they returned to earlier sources such as the patristics.[19] As the American Jesuit theologian John Courtney Murray took history seriously, he reinterpreted nineteenth-century papal teaching about church and state. Indebted to the earlier work of John Henry Newman, he argued for development of doctrine regarding religious liberty.[20]

Developments were shaped not only by attentiveness to history but also by dialogue with a modern philosophical perspective: existentialism. As theologians like Karl Rahner reflected on faith in dialogue with existential philosophy, they turned greater attention to faith as a response to God whose communication is not first and foremost information but is rather God's very self. This shifted the focus from the truths of faith to faith as the human response to God, who is the answer to the question that the human being is.[21] This emphasis on faith as a relational reality highlights *fides qua*.

Whereas the First Vatican Council issued a dogmatic constitution on faith, the Second Vatican Council issued one on revelation. *Dei Verbum* (Dogmatic Constitution on Divine Revelation) was not shaped by concerns about Enlightenment reason.[22] Revelation was not narrowed to propositions. Instead, *Dei Verbum* took seriously salvation history and focused on God's saving activity in history rather than on the divine attributes of God (DV 2–4). This document attends to the historical development of Scripture in the life of the Christian community (DV 8–9). Recognizing the interrelatedness of Scripture and tradition, the Second Vatican Council moved beyond the First Vatican Council's presentation of revelation in terms of two sources to a unitary focus on revelation as the Word of God.

The promulgation of *Dei Verbum* was a time of reconciliation. Pope Paul VI concelebrated Mass with theologians whose work the Vatican had judged negatively prior to the council, but the bishops of the Second Vatican Council then used to inform their own teaching. Among the concelebrants were John Courtney Murray and Henri de Lubac.[23] This Mass was a symbol of development in the church's reflection on faith. No longer in a defensive posture toward modernity, the Catholic bishops at the Second Vatican Council did not let Enlightenment challenges limit their teaching. Instead, they offered a more comprehensive presentation of revelation through a retrieval of the tradition informed by history and existential philosophy.

Faith and Revelation in the Wake of the Second Vatican Council

The reception of the Second Vatican Council's teaching about revelation has varied. As Catholics in the contemporary church interpret this council, some emphasize continuity and others emphasize development.[24] As a community that values tradition, the church has a strong inclination to emphasize continuity. As a community with a mission of proclaiming the Gospel in a changing world, the church attends to the activity of the Spirit in the church and in the world, leading to development. This tension between continuity and development shapes the life of the contemporary Catholic Church. Understandings of faith and revelation differ based on whether one emphasizes continuity with the First Vatican Council or development with the Second Vatican Council.

With regard to faith, those that emphasize continuity with the First Vatican Council are inclined to stress the potential confusion and divisions resulting from individual judgments about magisterial teaching. They tend to focus on revelation as propositional truth claims, and they understand a response of faith as assenting to those statements of faith, as Avery Dulles explains.[25] This perspective emphasizes scandal as dissent from doctrine.

In contrast, those that emphasize development with the Second Vatican Council are more likely to stress that the disciple is called to holiness and that revelation is God's saving activity in history. They are more likely to turn to Scripture as a written account of definitive revelation in the person of Jesus Christ and to spirituality as an experience of God's ongoing personal revelation in history. They are less likely to retrieve the language of scandal from the moral tradition. On the limited occasions they turn to the language of scandal, it is either to respond to the claim that dissent is a source of scandal or to attend to aspects of revelation that are a stumbling block, such as the incarnation and the cross.[26]

Spirituality, Scripture, and doctrine are all important sources for theology, for faith seeking understanding. When tensions exist among these sources, Catholics emphasize particular sources based on their understanding of revelation and faith. This sheds light on the reason the question of method has been so important in theology since the Second Vatican Council. Following Paul VI's 1968 teaching about artificial contraception in *Humanae Vitae*, tensions among sources (in particular, doctrine and experience) shaped many of the developments in theology that the Second Vatican Council invited. These developments serve as the backdrop for Pope John Paul II's formulation of a new profession of faith and an oath of fidelity in 1989.

Professions of Faith, Oaths of Fidelity, and Scandal

In the wake of the Second Vatican Council, Paul VI provided the church with an updated profession of faith.[27] The concerns from the Protestant Reformation incorporated into prior professions since Trent were removed, leaving the Nicene-Constantinopolitan Creed. Paul VI took this creed and elaborated on it. Nearly twenty years later, after public dissent by prominent theologians, such as Charles Curran and Hans Küng, regarding issues related to *Humanae Vitae*, John Paul II issued a new profession of faith.[28] This one returned to the Nicene-Constantinopolitan Creed and then added three paragraphs indicating that one assents to the church's dogma, holds its definitive doctrine, and submits to its authoritative teaching.

Ladislas Orsy invites reflection on the inclusion of definitive doctrine and authoritative teaching in a profession of faith, since they do not call for an assent of faith.[29] In addition, the paragraphs do not specify particular content of faith, which leaves a lack of clarity in the appropriate response in certain cases.[30] For instance, three preeminent theologians have differed on where to place the church's teaching about the nonordination of women: Francis Sullivan considers it authoritative teaching that would call for a response of submission; Joseph Ratzinger considers the same teaching definitive doctrine that must be held; and Avery Dulles considered it dogma that calls for an assent of faith.[31] In the apostolic letter *Ordinatio Sacerdotalis*, John Paul II did not define the Catholic position on the nonordination of women as infallible, but rather declared that the Catholic bishops dispersed throughout the world have taught definitively on this matter.[32] In response to this declaration, Francis Sullivan raised the question of evidence that the ordinary universal magisterium is in fact teaching this definitively.[33] Comments by members of the episcopate reinforce Sullivan's observation. For instance, Cardinal José da Cruz Policarpo of Portugal, who later retracted his comment under pressure from the Vatican, said that he saw no theological obstacle to ordaining women; and Bishop William Morris of Australia, who was removed by the Vatican after not retracting his statement, also spoke about the possibility of ordaining women.[34]

Nine years after John Paul II released this new profession of faith, he issued *Ad Tuendam Fidem* in response to theological dissent and specified a canonical penalty for not holding doctrine that has been taught definitively.[35] The 1989 profession of faith received attention again two decades after its release as the Vatican visitation of women's religious communities in the United States called for sisters on the visitation teams to make the profession of faith.[36] This raised the question of whether some would find John Paul II's version of the profession of faith an obstacle to professing their faith.

At the same time that John Paul II promulgated the 1989 profession of faith, he also issued an oath of fidelity. Like the profession of faith, the oath of fidelity is open-ended.[37] Not only has the nature of this oath been a source of concern but so too has the more basic decision to require oaths. Christians hear the Sermon on the Mount in which Jesus tells people not to take oaths but to say yes when they mean yes (Matt 5:33-37). Despite this, the rules of the community require oaths in certain cases. In a spirit that Donald Cozzens describes as "non-defensive, honest, and humble dialogue," he advocates, "Believers who practice their faith and publicly profess the creed of the church would no longer be required to take oaths of fidelity or make additional professions of faith before assuming church offices or before being called to the sacrament of orders. Attempts to enforce external compliance with doctrinal and ethical church teachings would be seen as contrary to the nature of faith and the role of conscience."[38] This observation not only challenges the contemporary use of oaths but also points to the nature of a profession of faith in its most authentic sense.

Understanding a profession of faith in terms of *lex orandi, lex credendi* (the rule of praying is the rule of believing) invites a return in focus to the liturgy where a member of the faith community professes one's shared faith with the community as an act of praising God. Resorting to the use of a profession of faith as an instrument to ensure loyalty and trust undermines the very purpose it is being used to serve. This use of the profession of faith can function as an obstacle to an authentic profession of one's faith in God.

Obstacles to Faith

Obstacles to faith take many forms. Obstacles associated with proclamation of the Gospel include language and ideas. Obstacles associated with living the Gospel include persecution and laws limiting religious practice. We will consider all of these.

Language as Stumbling Block to Faith

The community has tried to express the experience of God in conceptual form, as seen in professions of faith. This in turn provides language for those baptized into the community to name and interpret their experience of encountering God. The language is not God but rather a pointer toward and reflection of that encounter with God. The cataphatic tradition in Christian spirituality engages the analogical imagination by drawing on language from human experience to say something about God despite the inadequacies and limitations of using this language to name God. The apophatic tradition, which emphasizes that God is beyond our naming, reminds Christians not to limit God based on one's image of God. For instance, Jesus taught his disciples to pray by saying "Abba" (Father) (Matt 6:9). This draws on the human experience of fathers in order to say something about what God is like. Jesus, like the Hebrew Scriptures, also used female images to describe God (see, e.g., Luke 15:8-10). When Christians experience a feminine image of God challenging their paternal image of God, it is a reminder that God is Mystery.

Language, as well as its meaning, evolves over time. This affects the community's attempts to faithfully transmit God's revelation. For instance, the Nicene Creed mentioned above expresses the belief that for human salvation the Word became flesh. The Council of Nicaea refers to this with the Greek word ἐνανθρῶπήσαντα (from *anthrōpos*), and later Latin translations use the phrase *homo factus est*.[39] These words refer to human beings in a generic way and have been translated into English as "man." The meaning of the word "man" has evolved in contemporary English so that it is rarely used in a generic way but is rather used in a gender-specific way. After a liturgy in which the community professed the Nicene Creed, a man mistakenly made reference to the use of the word *vir* in the official Latin translation. He assumed the use of this gender-specific word for "man" in the original text when he heard the word "man." The English translation he heard was an obstacle to his appropriation of the community's faith, which understands the Word becoming flesh as salvific for all of humanity. In other words, the translation's use of the word "man" was a source of scandal.

The English translation of the institution narrative in the eucharistic prayer introduced in Advent of 2011 poses an obstacle to understanding Christ's sacrifice as salvific for all of humanity. For more than three decades, Catholics in the English-speaking world followed an International Commission on English in the Liturgy (ICEL) translation of the Sacramentary that used the word "all" to speak about Christ's sacrifice.[40] The new English translation of the Roman Missal from *Vox Clara* has changed this word to "many."[41] In an age of inclusion, this change sounds like an emphasis on exclusion. To the extent that the change is heard in this way, it poses an obstacle for the faith community as well as a crisis of conscience for presiders.

Language is an obstacle, at times, not only in speaking about God and God's activity but also in speaking about God's creation. One can observe this in the *Compendium of the Social Doctrine of the Church*, which provides a synthesis of Catholic social teaching's reflection on living biblical justice in our contemporary world.[42] Communicating the importance of human dignity and the injustice of discrimination, the text fails to be consistent in its use of inclusive language.[43] When Cardinal Renato Martino learned that this was an obstacle to the document's reception for some in the United States, he said that the United States Conference of Catholic Bishops could issue a more inclusive English translation for the next edition.[44] This reflects the importance of removing obstacles in order to proclaim the Good News more effectively.

Naming the experience of God in one's spiritual life, as well as in the community's liturgical life and work for biblical justice, provides an important basis for theological reflection for the life of the church. The contemporary Catholic Church is part of a two-millennia conversation about the meaning of God's revelation in the person of Jesus Christ. Theology involves a dialogue between past and present that values the interaction between the living tradition and the contemporary world.

Understandings of God as Stumbling Blocks to Faith

When an atheist states a lack of belief in God, one might inquire about the person's understanding of the god that does not exist. A Christian might respond that if God were understood in that way, the Christian too would not believe that *that* god exists. For unbeliever and believer alike, one's understanding of God can be an obstacle to faith in God. As Augustine perceptively notes, a person's idea of God is not God.[45]

At both an intellectual and an existential level, people often struggle with faith and its expression in the midst of suffering. The Wisdom literature in the Bible provides the faith community with such a story for reflection. In the story of Job, one hears of a faithful person's experience of the loss of blessings. His relationship with God is put to the test in these circumstances. While he remains faithful in the midst of his struggle with God, his friends judge that his suffering must be punishment for his sins. Based on their theology of divine retribution, they believe God rewards the just and punishes the wicked. They conclude that Job's suffering must be a punishment for sin. However,

Job declares his innocence (Job 1-14). The friends' ideas about God are obstacles to their encountering God in unexpected situations. To accept Job's experience that God allows innocent suffering would challenge their ideas about God's justice.[46]

The incarnation and crucifixion are even more profound challenges to ideas about God, particularly God's omnipotence. Christians proclaim that the Word became flesh and dwelled among us (John 1:14). God chose to enter the human condition and did so on the margins of the Greco-Roman world. From the beginning, Jesus experienced hardships. According to Scripture, he was not born in his parents' home in Nazareth but rather in a stable in Bethlehem (Luke 2:4-7). During his ministry, Jesus met resistance from religious leaders as he went throughout Galilee and Judea proclaiming and mediating the reconciling and liberating love of God's reign. Innocent of crimes, he unjustly died a criminal's death for this. That God would take on suffering and death, dying as an innocent victim, challenges ideas of an all-powerful God.

Both the incarnation and the crucifixion were stumbling blocks to faith for many Jews and Greeks with whom the disciples shared the Gospel. The Word becoming flesh challenged Judaism as a monotheistic faith. At the heart of this challenge is the act of believing in the Son of God when there is only one God. The Jews were awaiting an anointed one, a king like David. The sign on Jesus' cross that said "King of the Jews" draws attention to the incompatibility between the anticipated messiah and Christ crucified (Matt 27:37; John 18:33-40). The Greeks were challenged both by Christianity's claim that there is only one God and by the crucifixion of Christ. The gods of the Greco-Roman world were reverenced for their power and immortality. The suffering and death of Christ challenged their understanding of what a god is.

The experience of the risen Lord provides a new perspective on power and death. Christ revealed to the disciples that God's love is more powerful than sin and death. Disciples experienced this on the road to Emmaus and in the breaking of the bread, as well as when the risen Lord gave the disciples in Jerusalem the gift of peace to calm their fears (Luke 24:13-49). They experienced this as they proclaimed the reign of God in the midst of rejection and persecution. They remembered Jesus commissioning them to offer the gift of peace. If their peace was accepted, they were to stay. Otherwise, they were to move to the next town and offer the gift of peace (Luke 10:1-11).

Persecution as Stumbling Block to Faith

In the first centuries of Christianity, Roman governors at times required people to offer sacrifice to the emperor to demonstrate loyalty to the empire. The correspondence between Pliny, the governor of the province of Bithynia and Pontus in northern Asia Minor, and Trajan, the Roman emperor, provides a snapshot of this persecution at the beginning of the second century.[47] Pliny's letter highlights the large number of conversions to Christianity in his province, the diverse nature of the community, and the disruptive effects of Christian practices on social and economic life, as Christians did not worship at the pagan temples or buy meat that had been sacrificed there. Despite Pliny's edict against association, Christians gathered for prayer. When Christians were brought before him, he would acquit those who prayed to the Roman gods, offered a sacrifice to the emperor, and cursed Christ. Christians faced the temptation to renounce their faith by worshipping an idol to save their lives. Some did succumb to this temptation, and others refused to offer the sacrifice, resulting in imprisonment and even death.[48]

Preparation for baptism, for professing the Christian community's faith, was in many cases preparation for martyrdom, particularly after the emperor Severus outlawed conversion to Christianity in the Roman Empire in 202. At the beginning of the third century, Perpetua and other catechumens were arrested in Carthage. Perpetua's diary reveals that when she was brought before the governor, her father pressured her to offer a sacrifice for the emperor to save her life and her family's reputation. She refused. She and the other catechumens prepared for the death that would result from proclaiming to the governor that they were Christians. As a part of this preparation for martyrdom, they were baptized. As prisoners, they offered each other encouragement as they faced gruesome deaths by public execution. These public executions served as entertainment for the observers and as the ultimate form of evangelization by the martyrs.[49]

A few decades later, Carthage and the rest of the empire experienced persecution of Christians under Decius. This emperor issued a decree requiring that a sacrifice be offered and a certificate be obtained from a Roman official as evidence. Many Christians avoided this sacrifice by purchasing certificates indicating that they had offered the required sacrifice. Those imprisoned for refusing to offer the sacrifice were known as confessors. Those who failed to give witness to their faith, those who resorted to the purchase of certificates, approached the confessors seeking their forgiveness. They sought forgiveness for acting against the first commandment, "I am the LORD your God . . . ; you shall have no other gods before me" (Exod 20:2-3). They had experienced persecution as a stumbling block to faith, and they sought reconciliation with God and the community. The faithful witness of confessors and martyrs was not only a call to repentance for other Christians but also a call to conversion for non-Christians. Their witness invited others to experience the Good News of God's reign. They gave witness to the faith that Jesus had sent the apostles to share.[50]

Persecution of Christians continues into the twenty-first century. From minority communities in Muslim countries, like Iraq and Egypt, to underground communities in communist countries, like China and Vietnam, to small Christian communities in Latin American countries, like El Salvador and Brazil, Christians in recent decades have experienced violence, including torture and death, because of their faith.[51] In some cases the persecution is state sponsored. The types of states and the reasons for the sponsorship vary. Some states maintain that conversion to Christianity is a violation of Islamic law. Others maintain that Christians may not practice their faith in ways that have not been approved by the communist regime. Still others act because the economic interests of the elite in a capitalist nation are threatened by the Gospel's commitment to the poor. In other cases, religiously or economically motivated individuals or groups are the persecutors. Responding to these many sources of persecution, Pope Benedict XVI has reiterated the importance of the right to religious liberty, identifying it as a fundamental human right.[52]

Law as a Stumbling Block to Faith

Many stories of persecution of Christians from the early church as well as from the past century are vivid examples of laws as stumbling blocks to faith. A law against conversion that carries the death penalty is an obstacle to baptism. A law against gathering for Mass is an obstacle to receiving the Eucharist. Not only are laws that forbid or limit expressions of worship obstacles to faith but so too are laws that call for people to act in ways contrary to their "faith that does justice."[53] Catholics, as individuals and as a community, need to discern the particularities of God's call to participate in making God's reign present in our world. At times, Catholic individuals and institutions find the law an obstacle in responding to this call.

When a law is perceived as unjust and there is a possibility of changing the law, individuals and institutions can work for the needed change. When substantive change is not possible, exemption from the legal requirement to cooperate in the injustice through a conscience clause might be possible. While the Catholic moral tradition allows for the possibility of cooperation with an unjust law under certain circumstances, some Catholics have opposed any form of cooperation, raising the question of whether such cooperation compromises Catholics' witness to the Gospel.

Vatican II encouraged political participation and collaboration to promote the common good through reasoned dialogue about human rights. This tradition, which emphasizes the compatibility of faith and reason and defines law as "an ordinance of reason for the common good, made by [one] who has care of the community, and promulgated," was not inclined to identify law as a stumbling block to faith.[54] Yet, in the early 1990s the *Catechism of the Catholic Church* included laws as a source of scandal (CCC 2286). In the context of postmodernity, power receives greater attention than reason. Power is often exercised based on self-interest, whether individual or collective, rather than on the common good. In this context, there has been growing concern about the formation and implementation of laws and public policies that are contrary to Catholic values regarding human flourishing. As such laws require actions that compromise the values of Catholic individuals and institutions, Catholic leaders are placing greater emphasis on religious liberty.

Avoiding Scandal versus Moving beyond Scandal

We have considered language, ideas, persecution, and laws as stumbling blocks to faith. Language and ideas used to communicate about God are not adequate to the task and can result in confusion, but a Christian is not to avoid speaking about God because of the inadequacy of language or our inability to comprehend the incomprehensible. To move beyond this scandal, the community needs to continually seek to effectively communicate God's revelation in a given historical and cultural context. An absolute avoidance of scandal associated with language and ideas about God would result in a lack of evangelization. When faith is reduced to teaching, and when dissent from any teaching becomes a scandal, one will miss the invitation of the Holy Spirit to communicate God's reign in new ways. The virtue of humility and a life of prayer in a community of faith equip one to take steps beyond the scandal of the limits of language and ideas, as inadequate as those steps might be.

The suffering of persecution and the limitations of laws on living one's faith are challenges to Christian witness. The desire to avoid suffering and repression is natural. When avoiding these obstacles to faith becomes absolute, this natural desire leads to idolatry. Moving beyond scandal could take the form of experiencing the gift of Christ's presence in the midst of suffering, as the disciples on the road to Emmaus did. Restrictive laws invite attention to the ways in which the Spirit is guiding one's discernment of creative possibilities in limited situations as a way beyond scandal. Remembering the ways in which restrictive laws divided Christians in Carthage when Cyprian was bishop, we turn to the scandal of divisions in the church.

The Catholic Church and Scandal
CHAPTER 3

The eucharistic table, the place where the community gathers to give thanks, often serves as a reminder of the scandal of divisions among Christians and of incongruities between the faith disciples profess and the lives they lead. Christians who do not profess belief in the Real Presence of Christ in the Eucharist are excluded from receiving Communion at Mass.[1] Catholics who are divorced and remarried, whose lives do not reflect Catholic teaching about the indissolubility of marriage and who appear to sin through a choice contrary to the commandment against adultery, are likewise excluded.[2] At times, public figures have faced similar exclusion because of another's judgment of discontinuity between their public positions and Catholic teaching.[3] Segregationists in Louisiana, torturers in Chile, pro-choice politicians in the United States, gay rights advocates in the Netherlands, and a leader of Ordination of Catholic Women in Australia are among those who have been denied Communion.[4] Some church leaders deny Communion to avoid causing scandal, and others in the community take scandal at this. The Catholic Church as a community of faith and thanksgiving, a community of disciples, faces the challenge of discerning how best to witness to God's love in the world.

In this chapter we will begin with a brief overview of church as a community of faith and thanksgiving that has experienced the scandal of divisions. Attentive to divisions among Christian denominations and within the contemporary Catholic Church, we will compare the teachings about church from the First Vatican Council and from the Second Vatican Council. In light of ecclesial discourse that identifies dissent with scandal, we will give particular attention to church teaching and change. The Second Vatican Council's teaching about religious liberty sheds light on contemporary Catholic discourse about scandal, for the council's act of teaching challenges those tempted to equate dissent or change with scandal. Both the scandal of faithful discipleship and the scandal of discontinuity between the faith and the life of a disciple characterize the community of disciples. Grace and sin characterize not only the members of the community but also the community as a whole.

Church: A Community of Faith and Thanksgiving

The fullness of God's revelation in the person of Jesus Christ was first experienced and shared in the context of community. Jesus did not have only one follower but many. He did not send only one person to share the Good News of God's reign with others but many, and he tended to send them in pairs (Luke 10:1-2). The unconditional love his followers experienced was a love to be shared.

After Jesus' crucifixion, the community had reason to fear. In the midst of this fear, they experienced the risen Christ offering them peace and preparing them to proclaim the Good News even in the midst of resistance. In the midst of sorrow, the disciples on the road to Emmaus experienced Jesus as the Scriptures were broken open and as bread was broken and shared, as at the Last Supper before Jesus' crucifixion (Luke 24:13-35).

The risen Christ promised to send his Spirit, and the Spirit empowered the disciples to proclaim the reign of God throughout the Roman Empire and beyond (Acts 1:8). As people responded in faith to the proclamation of God's reign and chose to follow the Way, they were baptized into the community of believers. This evangelical community was also a eucharistic community. Members of the community would gather together to praise God in the celebration of the Lord's Supper, experiencing Christ's presence in the breaking of the bread. Members of the community would go forth from this eucharistic celebration empowered to love God and neighbor. As a Christian from one local church was visiting another, they recognized each other in their common profession of faith and in their participation in the Lord's Supper.[5]

The Gospel was proclaimed in many languages, and it spoke to the life experience of particular communities in different ways. These communities developed different customs as they celebrated the Eucharist, and the forms of leadership also varied. The Spirit united these diverse communities in their profession of faith and celebration of the Lord's Supper.[6] Those major cities of the Roman Empire where particular apostles gave witness to the faith took on prominence. Because of the witness given by Peter in Rome, the bishop of Rome took on the role of being "first among equals" in relationship to other bishops, who shared a common responsibility to foster unity both within one's own local church and among local churches.[7]

Despite the desire for unity in diversity, at times the diversity resulted in divisions. Divisions over expressions of faith, over the relationship between reconciliation and Eucharist, and over roles within the community posed obstacles in the community's life. From the first ecumenical council at Nicaea to the First Vatican Council, the leadership of the community of faith made judgments about conflicting expressions of faith. Prior to that, the community wrestled with whether one who chose to renounce the faith in the face of persecution could return to the eucharistic table.[8] From the schism between East and West to the Protestant Reformation, the community also divided over conflicting views of leadership for the community. In the wake of the Protestant Reformation, Robert Bellarmine emphasized the institutional nature of the Catholic Church, defining it as a community united in its profession of faith, reception of the sacraments, and guidance under the pope.[9] Divisions both within and among Christian communities are obstacles to the full embodiment of the church's identity as a community of faith and thanksgiving.

From Vatican I to Vatican II: Teaching about Church

The divisions among Christian communities shaped the First Vatican Council's teaching about church. As the council placed emphasis on the importance of unity, it did so with a focus on papal primacy. The fleeting reference to bishops, clergy, and the faithful simply serves as a reminder that each is to be united under the pope.[10] *Pastor Aeternus* (First Dogmatic Constitution on the Church of Christ) is almost exclusively about the pope. Such an emphasis on the pope creates the conditions for mistaking an important part of the church for the whole church.

The First Vatican Council exercised the highest level of teaching authority as it taught about papal infallibility.[11] This dogma of papal infallibility states that the pope can teach with the assistance of the Spirit on matters of faith and morals through definitions that are infallible (without error) and irreformable (without reversal). The one example of a papal definition since the First Vatican Council is the dogma on the assumption of Mary.[12] This expression of papal infallibility, as well as the actual teaching about papal infallibility, deepened the divide between the Catholic Church and other Christian denominations.

The First Vatican Council was in a defensive posture not only because of earlier changes in the life of the Christian church in the West but also because of the church's changing role in political life. From the losses of the French Revolution to the decline of the Papal States, the prominence and influence of the Catholic Church in the political world had diminished. Not long before the council, Pope Pius IX had identified separation of church and state as an error and advocated state support for the Catholic Church or, where that was not possible, religious liberty for the Catholic Church. The papacy's loss of considerable secular power and influence by the end of the nineteenth century was part of the context in which the bishops at Vatican I emphasized the authority of the pope in the Catholic Church.

With openness to the future rather than defensiveness from the past, the Second Vatican Council reflected in a more holistic way on the nature and mission of the church. Appreciating the church as mystery, they turned to biblical and theological language to name this reality.[13] In *Lumen Gentium* (Dogmatic Constitution on the Church), the bishops of the Second Vatican Council provided a rich array of names and descriptions for the church: people of God, Body of Christ, sacrament, holy and sinful, and pilgrim church, to name a few (LG 9, 7, 1, 8, 14, respectively). This language invites the community of faith not to mistake a part for the whole.

At times, people still equate the Catholic Church with the pope, but *Lumen Gentium* challenges this understanding of the faith community. In contrast with Vatican I's examination of church in terms of papal primacy, the bishops of the Second Vatican Council broadened the focus to all the faithful who enter the community through baptism. All of the baptized participate in the common priesthood, calling for a life of prayer, evangelization, and community. In this way those who are baptized into Christ participate in the work of Christ as priest, prophet, and king (cf. PA 1–3 and LG 10–13).

When the Second Vatican Council reflected on the hierarchy, it focused on the entire college of bishops rather than simply on the pope (LG 22–23). All of the bishops are ordained to serve as centers of unity for their respective local churches (dioceses) and as members of the college of bishops with responsibilities for the universal church. Through episcopal ordination, they have distinctive responsibilities for the sacramental life of the church, the preaching and official teaching of the church, and the organizational life of the church. Deacons and priests are ordained to support the bishop in his distinctive responsibilities reflective of Christ's ministries as priest, prophet, and king (LG 20–21, 28, 29). In this way *Lumen Gentium* offers a broader context in which to situate papal primacy by recalling other responsibilities of the pope, both as bishop of Rome and as head of the college of bishops (LG 18–29). Attentive to the teaching authority of the college of bishops, the council balanced Vatican I's emphasis on papal infallibility with its teaching about the ability of the bishops dispersed throughout the world to teach infallibly (LG 25).

Following the Second Vatican Council's teaching about collegiality, the number of episcopal conferences grew significantly. Underlying this teaching about episcopal collegiality are two different understandings of the nature of collegiality, one recognizing episcopal conferences as partial representations of the college, similar to regional councils, and the other simply recognizing a collegial spirit among local bishops. The latter view was adopted in Pope John Paul II's 1998 apostolic letter *Apostolos Suos* (On the Theological and Juridical Nature of Episcopal Conferences), emphasizing the authority of the local bishop and pope.[14] As Catholics note differences in teachings of bishops of neighboring dioceses, it raises questions and can pose an obstacle.

The focus on the church as institution and on the papacy after the Protestant Reformation reinforced differences between the Catholic Church and other Christian denominations. At the Second Vatican Council, rather than emphasize difference, the bishops highlighted the shared faith and history that unites Christians. The bishops recognized that divisions among Christian denominations pose an obstacle to faith. They wanted to overcome this scandal of a divided Body of Christ (Decree on Ecumenism [*Unitatis Redintegratio*] 1).

The Second Vatican Council wanted the community of disciples to address not only the scandal of divisions within the church but also the scandal of unjust divisions within the world. *Gaudium et Spes* (Pastoral Constitution on the Church in the Modern World) articulates the church's mission of proclaiming the Good News. If the *Syllabus of Errors* had offered condemnation of developments in the modern world, the Second Vatican Council recognized that the modern world is one in which a person encounters the goodness of creation, human sinfulness, and God's redeeming love (GS 2). In light of this, the church is to read the signs of the times and interpret them in light of the Gospel (GS 4). This mission is an essential dimension of what it is to be a eucharistic community. As the

Second Vatican Council's first document on liturgy and last
document on the mission of the church have informed the
life of the Catholic Church, the relationship between Eucharist and public life has received more attention than it did in
Gaudium et Spes (GS 38). At the Synod on the Eucharist forty
years after *Gaudium et Spes*, the bishops were more attentive to
the relationship between the Eucharist and the church's mission in the world.[15] They connected the Eucharist to the world's
struggles in the areas of reconciliation, migration of peoples,
and the environment, among others.[16]

From the perspective of the Second Vatican Council, dialogue, mutuality, and collaboration are to characterize life
within the church and its engagement with the world. These
are some of the virtues of the "spirit of Vatican II" that church
historian John O'Malley identifies through a careful analysis
of all of the council's texts.[17] Not all see these characteristics
as virtues. Some see dialogue, mutuality, and collaboration as
threats to the faith. These characteristics presuppose an openness to encounter or work with the other, which often invites
change. The underlying concern is that the encounter would
lead to compromise of, rather than growth in, one's faith. In
other words, it could lead to scandal. Those that emphasize
continuity rather than development as they interpret the Second Vatican Council are more likely to turn to the language
of scandal from the Catholic tradition. Their interpretation of
scandal, informed by the First Vatican Council's emphasis on
faith as believing doctrinal propositions, focuses on change in
teaching and dissent from teaching as obstacles to faith.

Church Teaching, Change, and Scandal

Sometimes language changes in order to faithfully communicate the tradition in a new context. Other times a new situation invites the retrieval of different sources from the tradition
in order to address a new context. Sometimes the community
wants to express an article of its faith in greater depth. These

types of change are often described generally as development.[18] The faith community prefers the language of development to that of change, since development is a particular form of change that remains faithful to the revelation of Jesus Christ under the guidance of the Holy Spirit.

The most challenging form of development, or change, is reversal. At the same time, one can point to examples of such reversal that are so commonly accepted by Christians that it can be hard to imagine that any Christians thought a particular practice was acceptable, such as slavery, or unacceptable, such as collecting interest on money.[19] Listening to Pope Benedict XVI teach about religious liberty in his World Day of Peace message in 2011, some would have been surprised to learn that Catholic teaching about religious liberty was quite different a half century earlier.[20] Prior to the Second Vatican Council, the Catholic Church advocated state support for the church rather than religious liberty for all; it no longer does.

In the years since the Second Vatican Council, some have responded negatively to a lack of change in church teaching, and others have responded negatively to change in church teaching. In the former case, many Catholics expected a reversal of the church's prohibition of artificial contraception, but that did not take place.[21] In the latter case, some have been challenged by a practical reversal of the tradition regarding the death penalty.[22] The contemporary emphasis on human dignity as a gift from God has reoriented practical advice from the Vatican about resorting to the death penalty as a way of protecting the common good.

One can note change not only in the content of teaching but also in a type of teaching. Commenting on *Ad Tuendam Fidem*, then-Cardinal Joseph Ratzinger introduced change into the category of definitive teaching so as to recognize change in the church's understanding of a particular teaching's nature.[23] With Vatican I's focus on teaching as propositions, the appropriate response was determined by the content of the teaching. The response called for by dogmas, teachings of faith necessary for salvation, was an assent of faith. Dogmas are infallible and ir-reformable, meaning they are without error and will not change. The tradition identified another type of teaching that is also without error and will not change: secondary objects of infal-libility. These teachings do not call for an assent of faith because they are not divinely revealed. Instead, they are teachings that are necessarily connected with divine revelation, and they are to be held definitively. By such a definition, a secondary object of infallibility cannot become a dogma because of the difference in type of content. In contrast, authoritative teaching, which calls for submission of mind and will, could come to be recognized by the community as a dogma. This would then call for an assent of faith.[24] In 1998 Ratzinger provided a more expansive interpretation of definitive teaching by including teaching that he identified as transitioning to the category of dogma. Two examples that he provided were teaching about the nonordi-nation of women and teaching prohibiting euthanasia.[25] These examples have contributed to ecclesial discourse about scandal.

There is change not only in terms of the categories of infal-libility; there is also a change regarding who teaches in this way. The primary source through the centuries has been ecumenical councils that have resolved disputed questions. Vatican I high-lighted another source: the pope. This council defined papal infallibility.[26] Some mistakenly think that this means the pope never makes an error. The point of the teaching, however, is to recognize that, at times, the pope teaches infallibly. The in-stances of this through the centuries have been relatively few.[27] To complement the teaching on papal infallibility, the Second Vatican Council taught about the ability of the bishops dispersed throughout the world to teach infallibly as the ordinary uni-versal magisterium (LG 25). This form of teaching infallibly is more common but less easily recognized as infallible. Normally, it is not until such teaching is challenged that there is a need for an ecumenical council (or pope) to define it. In light of this teaching about the ordinary universal magisterium, John Paul II made the novel move in *Ordinatio Sacerdotalis* (On Reserving

Priestly Ordination to Men Alone) and *Evangelium Vitae* (On the Value and Inviolability of Human Life) of declaring that the ordinary universal magisterium had taught infallibly about the nonordination of women, abortion, and euthanasia.[28]

The Second Vatican Council reflected on the relational nature of teaching as it recognized the role of reception in the teaching process. The Holy Spirit is guiding the whole church in its response of faith to God's revelation.[29] The lack of reception of a teaching calls for discernment about the work of the Spirit in that situation. We now turn to such a situation in which the Spirit assisted the church in the development of its teaching.

Change in Teaching: Religious Liberty

Addressing the College of Cardinals, the Roman Curia, and then the world at the beginning of a new year, Pope Benedict repeatedly advocated the right to religious freedom as a central human right.[30] He did this within days of the forty-fifth anniversary of the Second Vatican Council's Declaration on Religious Liberty, *Dignitatis Humanae*. In his World Day of Peace message, Benedict made this remarkable statement: "Religious freedom is at the origin of moral freedom."[31] From lack of recognition of religious liberty as a human right to advocating religious freedom as a central human right, Catholic thought about religious liberty changed. Were John Courtney Murray, the primary drafter of *Dignitatis Humanae,* alive to hear Pope Benedict, he would have reason to marvel at such significant change in Catholic teaching about religious liberty in a half century.

In the nineteenth century, the *Syllabus of Errors* had condemned the separation of church and state.[32] The Catholic position regarding church-state relations was that the Catholic Church should receive the support of the state, and where that was not possible the Catholic Church should be granted religious liberty. This was known as thesis-hypothesis. This position did not advocate religious liberty for those who were not Catholic. The rationale for this was "error has no rights."[33]

The American Jesuit theologian John Courtney Murray, analyzing the teaching of Pope Leo XIII regarding this position, determined that this teaching was a response to historical conditions in Europe during the nineteenth century.[34] He was able to arrive at this conclusion by examining the way in which the doctrine of church-state relations had developed in light of historical circumstances. During the 1940s and 1950s Murray argued for doctrinal development in the church's teaching about religious liberty. Because Catholic teaching about religious liberty was thought to be infallible, John Courtney Murray was silenced on the question. When he could no longer examine the church's understanding of the relation between church and state, he examined the American understanding of the relation between church and state. In 1960, a number of his essays on the topic were collected into a book titled *We Hold These Truths*.[35] All of this work informed the contributions he made as a theological adviser at the Second Vatican Council at the invitation of Cardinal Francis Spellman.

At the Second Vatican Council, the bishops, attentive to the denial of religious freedom as a threat to human dignity, read this sign of the times in a way that led them to retrieve passages from Scripture that spoke to the question of religious liberty and to develop the church's teaching on this topic (DH 11–12). Influenced by the work of European theologians, the reasoning shifted from rights residing in truth to rights residing in the human person. One of those rights grounded in the dignity of the human person is religious liberty. This right allows people to pursue the truth, to pursue God. The exercise of this right does not necessarily imply success in one's pursuit, but it is a condition for that possibility. Influenced by John Courtney Murray, drawing on the American experience, they recognized the importance of including the state's role of safeguarding public order (DH 2).

Church: A Community of Disciples

At the same time that the Second Vatican Council taught about religious liberty, it also taught about the church's mission in the world. *Gaudium et Spes* begins by identifying the church as a community of disciples sharing the Good News with the world (GS 1). This sharing takes place not only through the words one professes but also through the life one lives. The bishops were attentive to failures in the life of discipleship posing an obstacle for others (GS 43). With that in mind, we will focus on the witness of a diverse community of disciples.

Living the Gospel message of God's reign begins with experiencing God's love and responding with God's grace to the invitation to live the Good News. Disciples are invited to "fall in love [with God], stay in love and it will decide everything," as Pedro Arrupe says.[36] God leads disciples to love God and neighbor in different ways. At the same time, there are distinctive characteristics that others will expect of Christians, based on the biblical vision and the faith Christians profess. For instance, they will notice whether one responds to one's enemies with love. They will recognize whether the Lord is truly central in one's life or whether wealth, status, power, security, reputation, or popularity is more central to one's identity. Others will observe how one's relationship with the risen Lord affects one's relationship to death, whether one's own or that of others. Not only are the disciples' failures an obstacle to faith for others, but so too can be the faithful practices of Christians as they offer evangelical witness. As Christians appropriate the Gospel in different ways, the witness takes various forms. This diversity threatens some. At times, this leads people to focus on difference and use this as a basis for exclusion. A truly catholic (or universal) church, however, appreciates difference. In this spirit, we turn to the witness given by five Catholics since the Second Vatican Council that has profoundly influenced the imagination of Catholics in different ways.

Dorothy Day was a convert to Catholicism after she overcame the obstacle of Christians failing in their witness to the Gospel.

She wanted her daughter, born of a common-law marriage to an atheist father, to be baptized. She chose to enter the Catholic Church as well. She saw Christ in the hungry that she fed in the Catholic Worker houses she founded. She lived among and cared for the poor in the United States during the Great Depression and subsequent decades. She witnessed love of enemies by opposing wars, from World War II to Vietnam. She was imprisoned for her pacifist activities. The Sermon on the Mount and the parable of the sheep and the goats captured her imagination (Matt 5–7; 25:31-46). Her actions reflected values found there.[37]

Mother Teresa also saw Christ in those who were suffering and responded to their needs. She was a religious sister who first went to India as a missionary to work as an educator. She left the comfort of life at the school to live among the destitute and to respond to the needs of the sick and the hungry. As a Christian in India, she gave witness to a relationship with God that was understood in terms quite different from that of other religious believers in such a religiously diverse country. Others joined her, and she founded the Sisters of Charity. Her relationship to public authorities was less confrontational than that of Dorothy Day, and world leaders listened when she spoke on behalf of the life of the unborn or the death row inmate.[38]

Cardinal Joseph Bernardin of Chicago also offered a powerful witness to a life lived as a response to grace. He did this from a position of leadership within the US Catholic Church. He significantly shaped its engagement with the world after Vatican II. From advocating peace in Vietnam to development and participation through the Catholic Campaign for Human Development to protection for the unborn, he promoted respect for life across the continuum. As Bernardin articulated a consistent ethic of life, he invited a divided church and nation to embrace a Gospel vision of justice and peace. During the nuclear arms race of the Cold War, he led a dialogue about promoting peace. This resulted in the 1983 pastoral letter The Challenge of Peace: God's Promise and our Response, which was both a reflection of and a contribution to that dialogue.[39] He participated in ecumenical and interreligious initiatives. He responded with love of enemy when he was falsely accused of sexually abusing a seminarian. In *The Gift of Peace*, he gave witness to trust in the risen Lord as he was dying of cancer.[40] Like Bartolomé de las Casas, a sixteenth-century Dominican missionary during the Spanish conquest of America, Bernardin knew that the only way to proclaim the Gospel is with peace and through persuasion.[41] In a spirit of reconciliation, Bernardin, just days before his death, advocated dialogue in the US Catholic Church through the Catholic Common Ground Initiative.[42] In response to this, he met public resistance from other prominent US cardinals.[43]

Archbishop Oscar Romero of San Salvador also met resistance from his fellow bishops as he gave witness to the Gospel message. Following the murder of Father Rutilio Grande, SJ, and the lack of government response, he engaged in a public action that other bishops did not favor. He closed the Catholic schools for three days and tried to unite Catholics in prayer with only one Mass at the cathedral the following Sunday. This reflected his solidarity with the pastoral workers of the Archdiocese of San Salvador in making a preferential option for the poor. This preferential option for the poor was a choice to enter into solidarity with the poor to protest poverty and, in so doing, to witness to God's concern for the poor. Romero challenged the oppressive conditions of poverty and the repressive government actions used to maintain it. He protested these human rights violations. When asked about the death threats he received, Romero's response exemplified love of enemies. The words of Mexican bishop Don Samuel Ruiz, "There are some who want to make themselves enemy to me, but I have no enemies," could just as easily have been spoken by Romero.[44] He loved the wealthy and the poor alike; at the same time, this love challenged the status quo in which a small number of wealthy families owned most of the land in the country and the poor struggled to survive. Based on the Gospel, he preached many homilies that called for changing this social reality through an end to the human rights violations that were employed. Finally, the military had heard enough. In response to Romero's homily calling for them to stop killing their brothers and sisters, they assassinated him as he presided at Mass the next day, March 24, 1980.[45]

Pope John Paul II came not from the experience of a capitalist system maintained by violence but from a communist system maintained by violence. Under an atheistic totalitarian regime in Poland, Karol Wojtyla led a persecuted church as bishop of Krakow before becoming Pope John Paul II. He was well positioned to support the solidarity movement in the Gdansk shipyard that chipped away at communism's hold in Eastern Europe and eventually resulted in democracy in those countries. He promoted peace as he visited nation after nation, sharing the Gospel message.[46] He gave witness to love of enemy when he forgave the man who had attempted to assassinate him.[47] Like Bernardin, he wanted his experience of the dying process to be an affirmation of faith.[48]

These five Catholic icons give witness to living their relationships of faith in God in different ways. The context shapes the expression of faith, even as common gospel themes run through their witness. Icons, so common in Eastern Christianity, draw one past the image toward the divine. In similar fashion, these holy lives invite one to a deeper relationship with God and to a life that gives unique witness to God's reign. To say that they are holy is not to say that they are without sin, and both their holiness and their sinfulness can be an obstacle to others.

Disciples are called to live their faith by witnessing the Good News of God's reign. For some, this witness means choosing a communal life of poverty, celibacy, and obedience for the sake of proclaiming the Gospel. For others, it means forming a domestic church in which the family witnesses to God's love in and for the world. In the midst of multiple identities, such as worker, consumer, citizen, family member, and friend, one's identity as disciple needs to permeate them all. God recognizes the ways in which fear, anxiety, and disordered desires can be obstacles to living the Good News, and in response to the question in the Gospel of Matthew about why Jesus is so focused on sinners, Jesus indicates that he has come for those who are in need of his healing (Matt 9:12). God continues to offer the gift of grace to enable all to live in right relationship with God and others. The choices that disciples make in response to this grace affect the degree to which their lives will be a witness to God's reign or a scandal because of the incongruity between the faith they profess and the lives that they live. Disciples are empowered for this mission of giving witness to God's reign when they gather as a community to give thanks to God and receive nourishment from the Word and the Eucharist. They are sent forth from Mass as members of a church in the midst of change to engage a world in the midst of change.

Dialogue in a Divided Church

The church has experienced the scandal of divisions over belief and practice from its earliest days, according to the Pauline letters and the Acts of the Apostles. To move beyond the scandal of division, Christians need the grace of Christ to foster a reconciling spirit within the community. Gathering together in Christ's name and giving thanks to God together provide a basis for dialogue, an exchange of words, and a shared discernment regarding the presence of the Word. Ecumenical dialogue among Christians of different denominations and dialogues among US Catholics sponsored by the Catholic Common Ground Initiative are efforts to move beyond the scandal of division.[49] Such efforts meet resistance as some attempt to avoid scandal that could result from such dialogue, whether from confusion or from the compromise of truth. When the approach to avoiding such scandal is an absolute avoidance of dialogue, the choice maintains the current scandal of a divided Body of Christ.

Since Christians are divided over leadership, John Paul II issued *Ut Unum Sint* (On Commitment to Ecumenism) to foster ecumenical conversation.[50] Even as Christians discuss division over papal leadership, Christian communities remain divided over, and in some cases silent about, female clergy, homosexual clergy, and married clergy. The Catholic Church prohibits or restricts all three. John Paul II said that the Catholic Church does not have the authority to ordain women, that this has been taught infallibly by the ordinary universal magisterium, and that this is not open for dialogue.[51] Under the pontificate of Benedict XVI, as Catholic seminaries in the United States were under investigation because of the clerical sexual abuse scandal, the Vatican released a statement on the inadmissibility of persons with homosexual tendencies to the priesthood.[52] As married Anglican priests, opposed to developments in their community such as acceptance of female and openly gay bishops, converted to Roman Catholicism, the Vatican has allowed for such converts to serve as married Roman Catholic priests. At the same time, the Catholic Church maintains the discipline of not ordaining other married men in the Roman Rite, though it does in other rites.

The prohibition against ordaining married men as Roman Catholic priests was a response a millennium ago to the scandal of misappropriation of church property for their descendants. This approach to avoiding scandal has reduced the number of potential candidates for the Roman Catholic priesthood and contributes to the lack of priests for sacramental ministry in parishes. The scandal of misappropriation of church property continues to this day and invites reflection on how to effectively move beyond such financial scandals. Addressing this through structures of external accountability that reduce the opportunity for dishonest use of power would be a more effective approach to moving beyond financial scandals.

The Congregation for Catholic Education's effort to avoid scandal by excluding homosexual men from the seminary creates an obstacle for those homosexual men God might call to the priesthood and for the community they would serve. After stating the need for respect and sensitivity, as well as for no unjust discrimination, toward those with homosexual tendencies, the congregation fails to demonstrate this as it asserts the inability of homosexual men to relate appropriately to others and the potential risk of ordaining them. Rather than an absolute exclusion of those with homosexual tendencies from seminaries, each candidate needs to be evaluated regarding his suitability for ordained ministry, since the necessary virtues, such as chastity, are to be found in both heterosexual and homosexual candidates for the priesthood.

The exclusion of women from ordained ministry poses an obstacle both within the Catholic community and among Christian communities. To those who judge this policy unjust discrimination, the Vatican denies the charge, asserting that priestly service is rooted not in a right but in a vocation. To avoid the scandal of confusion, church leadership has closed dialogue on this subject. Moving beyond this scandal will require courage for the church to enter into dialogue and truly discern whether God might be calling women to this service. Such discernment will call for humility because our ideas of God are not God, and Christians need to avoid the scandal of making one's idea about God's activity into an idol.

While there are policies in place that prohibit or restrict the ordination of women, married men, and homosexual men, only in the first case is it a matter of doctrine with a papal declaration asserting that the bishops are teaching infallibly. It is worth noting that the pope did not invoke papal infallibility to teach this and that bishops have expressed positions that suggest they are not teaching this infallibly. One might ask whether the silence imposed on the church is like the silence imposed on John Courtney Murray, a silence that bore fruit in *Dignitatis Humanae* (Declaration on Religious Liberty).

Societal Change, Catholic Teaching, and Scandal
CHAPTER 4

When the bishops of the Second Vatican Council returned to their local churches, many observed social movements working to change society. Colonies sought liberation from colonial powers. The poor sought liberation from oppressive living conditions. African Americans sought liberation from racial discrimination. Women sought liberation from sexual discrimination. The peace movement opposed war and the nuclear arms race. Social movements also worked to change societies' views about the death penalty, euthanasia, and abortion. The population control movement opposed growth in the population, given the earth's limited resources. The sexual revolution advanced changes in laws related not only to reproduction, such as those limiting access to contraceptives and abortion, but also to marriage, such as those restricting divorce. These were times of change, and the church was eager to be in dialogue with this world of change, for the church has a mission to proclaim the Good News in this context.

In this chapter, we will examine the interactions between particular social movements and Catholic teaching that exemplify the dynamic of "reading the signs of the time and interpreting them in the light of the Gospel."[1] Social movements often rely on the dynamic of sociological scandal in an effort to change both culture and law, and sometimes they challenge theological scandal, while other times they contribute to it. In other words, at times movements invite greater commitment to the Gospel, such as practices to overcome the scandal of inequality, while at other times their ends or means conflict with the Gospel vision of human flourishing. Often Christians differ in their evaluations of a particular movement, and among Catholics those emphasizing continuity with the First Vatican Council rather than development with the Second Vatican Council are more inclined to retrieve the language of scandal for those changes judged contrary to God's dominion or the will of Christ.

Societal Change and Catholic Teaching

As disciples share the Gospel through lives of service, they often encounter situations of injustice that call for change. As they join with others to improve the situation, they may find themselves working with others who have very different values and visions. The disciple needs to be attentive to the way in which collaboration promotes and/or compromises the realization of God's reign. Attentive to the way in which both the magisterium and Catholic activists have used the language of scandal in relationship to particular issues, we will examine Catholic teaching as it responds to some of those movements. In light of *Gaudium et Spes*'s identification of poverty and social inequality as scandalous, we turn to three liberation movements from that time.

Liberation Movements and Catholic Teaching

Jesus came to proclaim Good News to the poor and liberty to captives (Luke 4:16-21). As the church participates in Christ's mission, it too is called to deepen its commitment to the poor. *Gaudium et Spes* (Pastoral Constitution on the Church in the Modern World), following the lead of Pope John XXIII, invited precisely that by calling for solidarity with the poor (see, e.g., GS 1). As the Latin American bishops returned from the Second Vatican Council, poor Christians working for liberation as an expression of faith informed the bishops' reflection.[2] This laid the groundwork for their teaching at the meeting of the Latin American Episcopal Conference (CELAM) in Medellin in 1968, which developed the teaching of *Gaudium et Spes* on the scandal of poverty.[3] Gustavo Gutiérrez named well the obstacle to faith that poverty poses. He draws attention to the challenge of proclaiming a God of life in the midst of "unjust and premature death."[4] In order to make the Good News credible, he, like many others, entered into solidarity with the poor. This solidarity includes protest against the unjust conditions in which the poor live. He, like many others, has given witness to God's preferential love for the poor by making a preferential option for the poor.[5]

Before this theological reflection on the preferential option for the poor was received as a gift for the universal church in Pope John Paul II's apostolic letter *Sollicitudo Rei Socialis* (On Social Concern), the Congregation for the Doctrine of the Faith raised concerns about liberation theology because of its use of Marxist social analysis.[6] The Vatican held that it was not possible to separate Marxist social analysis from Marxist ideology, which was atheistic and advocated violent revolution.[7] The Vatican was well aware of communism as an obstacle to faith and emphasized this obstacle to faith to a greater degree than that of capitalism. The Second Vatican Council, however, had invited a more comprehensive consideration of poverty (including that resulting from capitalism) as a source of scandal.[8] Recalling Christ's mission of bringing Good News to the poor had deepened the church's commitment to solidarity with the poor and marginalized, reminding the church that "[e]xcessive economic and social disparity between individuals and peoples of the one human race is a source of scandal" (GS 29). It was precisely these excessive economic differences that CELAM responded to in its teachings and invited the church to respond to in its practices. Through this, the church in Latin America began to change its alignment with the wealthy and powerful to solidarity with the poor.

Some have noted with disappointment that at the November 2011 meeting of the United States Conference of Catholic Bishops, the conference did not choose to reflect theologically on Occupy Wall Street's message highlighting the economic disparity between the wealthiest 1 percent of the population and the other 99 percent of the population.[9] While the US bishops did not choose to teach more about economic justice and the preferential option for the poor on the twenty-fifth anniversary of their pastoral letter Economic Justice for All, the Vatican did release a teaching document in response to the global financial crisis.[10] This carries on the tradition of teaching about economic justice found in the nineteenth-century papal encyclical *Rerum Novarum* (The Condition of Labor) that expressed concern for the poor through theological reflection on the labor movement during the Industrial Revolution.[11]

The recognition of social difference as a potential source of scandal has supported engagement with those experiencing discrimination on the basis of race and sex. In the United States, African Americans were struggling for civil rights. In the South, they were working to overcome a system of segregation that developed after the abolition of slavery in the nineteenth century. Under this system, African Americans did not have the opportunity to attend the same schools, eat at the same lunch counters, ride in the same part of the bus, or use the same restrooms as those of European descent. They also did not have the same opportunity to vote. Few would have imagined that four decades after the assassination of Martin Luther King Jr. the United States would elect a president of African descent.[12] In Forming Consciences for Faithful Citizenship, the US Catholic bishops' 2007 statement on political responsibility, the conference chose to identify racism as an example of an intrinsic evil.[13] The media's coverage of Hurricane Katrina had been a reminder of the strong correlation between race and poverty, a reality that Catholic Charities encounters in its ministry and wrote about in Poverty and Racism: Overlapping Threats to the Common Good.[14]

African Americans have experienced racism not only in society but also in the Catholic Church. Historically, this ranged from religious communities holding slaves to a system of segregation in churches after emancipation.[15] Sometimes the segregation of Catholic churches in the United States was by church building, whereas other times it was by location within the church, as African Americans were required to sit in the balcony. One could find segregation in seminary education and religious communities as well.[16]

The movement for racial justice challenged inequality in society, including the Catholic Church's participation in this unequal system. The desegregation of schools informed the US Catholic bishops' 1958 teaching on race relations.[17] A decade later, after race riots in major US cities, the bishops once again reflected on race relations.[18] Protest against social inequality rooted in race invited the church to deepen its commitment to the Gospel. Reflecting on this liberation movement in light of the Gospel, one recalls Jesus in solidarity with those on the margins of society. This challenges Christians to work for structural justice that does not privilege any race. Racial discrimination in the church needs to be challenged by recalling Paul's message that baptism makes Christians one in Christ. The movement for racial equality invites disciples to deepen their Gospel commitment to transformation of society and to conversion in the church.

Similarly, discrimination based on sex also calls for transformation of society and conversion in the church. In many Western countries, women were seeking greater opportunities for participating in and contributing to the common good. Often women found that opportunities for education, employment, and land ownership were limited because of gender and marital status. Social structures made many women dependent on men and subject to their control. In more extreme cases, women were treated as property and experienced domestic violence. Stories of Jesus interacting with women were ones of Good News and hope. The retrieval of these stories, however, occurs within a faith community, which has not faithfully communicated the goodness of God's creation in its evaluation of women through the centuries. These failures of the faith community can pose an obstacle to women hearing the Good News of Christ's love for them.

The 1971 Synod of Bishops understood well the need for reflection on the place of women in society and in the church.[19] It recognized that to proclaim justice, the church needs to be a witness of justice, and it called for the formation of committees to examine the place of women in the church and in society.[20] The next year, Pope Paul VI reformed minor orders to allow laymen to be lectors and acolytes.[21] In so doing, an effort to increase lay participation resulted in new forms of sexual discrimination against women.

In 1976 the Congregation for the Doctrine of the Faith responded to the ordination of women within some Protestant denominations, for these ordinations raised the question of whether the Roman Catholic Church in an age of ecumenism would also ordain women. Interestingly enough, it had already done so in communist Czechoslovakia in 1970; Bishop Felix Davidek ordained Ludmila Javorova for the underground Roman Catholic Church.[22] Davidek was not able to travel to Rome to discuss with Pope Paul VI this pastoral response to the needs of a persecuted church, and six years later in *Inter Insigniores* (Declaration regarding the Question of the Admission of Women to Ministerial Priesthood) the Congregation for the Doctrine of the Faith stated that the church does not have the authority to ordain women.[23] In addition, it offered explanations for the nonordination of women, including one based on Jesus' choice of apostles. In the years following that statement, the work of Scripture scholars, church historians, and theologians highlighted deficiencies in the arguments and demonstrated the open nature of the question.[24]

A few years after *Inter Insigniores*, the US and Canadian Catholic bishops approved the use of gender-inclusive language in the liturgy, but the Vatican did not authorize its use.[25] Bishop Donald Trautman explains that this refusal is because of pressure by some American Catholics who insist that gender-inclusive language in the liturgy will lead to the ordination of women, a claim that Trautman rejects.[26] In 1994 the Vatican officially allowed dioceses to determine on an individual basis whether to have altar girls.[27] Lest this be perceived as a step toward further change, the Vatican issued *Ordinatio Sacerdotalis* (On Reserving Priestly Ordination to Men Alone), which states that the church cannot change its teaching on the nonordination of women and that the ordinary universal magisterium teaches that this must be held definitively.[28]

In anticipation of the United Nations' Fourth World Conference on Women, John Paul II wrote a Letter to Women.[29] This 1995 letter called for change in society to recognize human rights that women are often denied, and John Paul II recognized that the nonordination of women makes the Catholic Church susceptible to criticism. Anticipating this, John Paul II offered his explanation of why he did not consider the nonordination of women a form of unjust discrimination.[30]

For some, the nonordination of women remains an obstacle to faith. Others take scandal at women assuming the leadership roles that have been approved in the church.[31] Critical of the feminist movement for creating tensions between men and women, the Congregation for the Doctrine of the Faith advocated a new feminism and collaboration between men and women in a 2004 statement.[32] In 2010 the publication of canonical penalties identifying both clerical sexual abuse of minors and the ordination of women in the same way as "more grave delicts" was a source of scandal as members of the faith community struggled with the apparent identification of two very different acts.[33] Roy Bourgeois, a Maryknoll priest, has been threatened with both excommunication and expulsion from his religious order for his role in the ordination of a woman. He chose to participate in the ordination service because of his conviction that one must work for justice in order to promote peace.[34] He is best known for his work in raising awareness of US complicity in both the Salvadoran civil war and, particularly, the assassination of the University of Central America Jesuits who had made a preferential option for the poor and worked to promote peace.

Peace Movements and Catholic Teaching

Reflecting on the Sermon on the Mount's command to love one's enemies and the witness of early Christians who refused to serve in the military, some Catholics have felt a call to be conscientious objectors to war. During World War II, there were very few Catholic pacifists, but Dorothy Day and the Catholic Workers were. Following World War II, Pax Christi formed first in Europe and then beyond. The number of Catholic pacifists grew.[35]

At the beginning of the Second Vatican Council, John XXIII negotiated a peaceful end to the Cuban Missile Crisis.[36] Attentive to the need for peace, he advocated human rights: civil and political, as well as social and economic. In so doing, he echoed the United Nations' Universal Declaration of Human Rights.[37] In the wake of the human rights abuses associated with World War II, this declaration was a practical agreement to promote human dignity.

Since at least the time of Augustine, the Catholic tradition has recognized that love of neighbor and protection of the common good could lead one to engage in war. In an effort to limit the resort to war and the destruction in war, the just war tradition developed. In *Gaudium et Spes*, the bishops recognize not only this means of working for peace but also conscientious objection to war, provided one serves the common good in another way (GS 79). In 1983 the National Conference of Catholic Bishops presented both pacifism and the just war theory as legitimate ways for Catholics in the United States to promote peace.[38] The pacifist position provides a countercultural witness; the just war theory provides a means to temper the impulse to go to war, even as it is susceptible to being co-opted for political ends.[39] The pastoral letter The Challenge of Peace: God's Promise and Our Response not only held together two approaches that exist in tension with each other; it also fostered dialogue about nuclear deterrence and disarmament. This dialogue occurred not only in the US Catholic Church and US society but also among some other national episcopal conferences. In fact, representatives from a number of conferences gathered in Rome to discuss the differences in their prudential judgments.

Just months before the terrorist attacks of September 11, 2001, and the *Boston Globe* coverage of clerical sexual abuse in January 2002, Catholic ethicist Margaret Farley talked about the Catholic Church in public life in terms of the "scandal of compromised credibility."[40] This description became all the more applicable as clerical sexual abuse and inadequate responses to it became known. Because of the Catholic Church's failure to prevent the violence of clerical sexual abuse, US society was less inclined to hear the US Catholic bishops evaluate actions in Afghanistan in 2002 and the invasion of Iraq in 2003. Their continued advocacy for a peaceful response to the violence of the terrorist attacks on the World Trade Center and the Pentagon lacked the moral authority their advocacy once had.[41]

Pro-Life Movements and Catholic Teaching[42]

The twentieth century saw movements in many countries to abolish capital punishment. Activists asked why the state kills in order to teach its citizens not to kill. They argued that capital punishment does not truly promote the common good by protecting society. The arguments have borne fruit in new laws abolishing capital punishment in any number of countries. Even where it has not been abolished, injustice in the application of the punishment has at times led to a moratorium.

The Catholic tradition has allowed the use of capital punishment to protect the common good. Theological arguments that understand the sacredness of human life in terms of God's dominion over life and death have justified capital punishment based on God's delegation of authority to the state in certain circumstances.[43] As the understanding of the sacredness of human life has developed with a focus on the intrinsic dignity of the human person created in the image and likeness of God, it calls for all human life to be respected, both that of the innocent and that of the guilty. As societies recognize human dignity as intrinsic, they develop ways to protect the common good without destroying human life. In *Evangelium Vitae* (On the Value and Inviolability of Human Life), John Paul II says that he cannot imagine a situation today in which capital punishment would be necessary to protect the common good (EV 56). Some might dismiss this as John Paul II's prudential judgment, but it also reflects a larger transition in the magisterium's theological understanding of the sacredness of human life. As such, the teaching about capital punishment appears to be in transition.[44]

Not only has a pro-life movement worked to protect the lives of the guilty, but such movements have also responded to social movements that allow for the killing of the innocent. With a concern about quality of life for the ill and the elderly, some consider killing a form of compassion and appropriate the language of dignity to argue for euthanasia. Responding to the death with dignity movement, laws have changed in some jurisdictions, such as that of the Netherlands to allow euthanasia and that of the state of Oregon in the United States to allow physician-assisted suicide.[45] A pro-life movement has responded by pointing to the way in which hospice addresses quality of life by treating pain without killing the patient. This pro-life movement has also raised the question of how a physician's assistance in a patient's suicide affects the virtues needed by a health-care provider.

Catholic teaching classifies euthanasia and physician-assisted suicide as the direct taking of innocent human life and therefore intrinsically evil (EV 65–66). To identify something as intrinsically evil does not reflect the gravity of the action, though in this case it is grave indeed.[46] Rather, it indicates that regardless of additional circumstances and intentions, it will remain evil because it is evil in and of itself. For instance, the apparent goods of exercising autonomy or free choice in choosing death or of desiring to end the suffering of another do not in fact change an evil action to a good one. Euthanasia and physician-assisted suicide remain evil. This judgment does not lead to the conclusion that every possible means must be used to prolong life. Extraordinary or disproportionate means may be omitted. It is for precisely this reason that ethicists have debated whether artificial nutrition and hydration in particular cases should be classified as ordinary or extraordinary care.[47] Recent magisterial teaching has classified it as ordinary care.[48]

In response to public concerns about issues at the end of life, the church engages in the public argument regarding what human dignity requires. This can be done based on reason alone. A relationship of faith in God, though, allows for a greater possibility of not acting out of a fear that seeks control, whether a control that kills in order to end suffering or a control that prolongs life at all costs.

In societies that evaluate human worth in terms of productivity, not only are the elderly and infirm vulnerable but so too are the young who are dependent. As societies discriminated against women because of their children or ability to have children and as women sought greater opportunities to contribute to the common good, the organizations in the movement for women's rights often adopted a reproductive rights position that included abortion. As the population control movement tried to limit the planet's population, abortion was a means to its end. These movements were ready to enter into a coalition with the abortion rights movement.[49]

Prior to the Second Vatican Council, most noncommunist countries had very restrictive, if any, legal allowance for abortion.[50] For instance, a doctor might be legally allowed to perform an abortion to save a woman's life. During the past half century, countries have considered other possible exceptions, such as cases of rape and incest, fetal abnormality, and health of the mother. With regard to health of the mother, the question of how to define it and who evaluates it varies from country to country.[51] Abortion laws in many countries have changed during the past fifty years, resulting in the killing of many young lives in utero. In addition to this, embryos are also being killed in laboratories as excess embryos are created from in vitro fertilization procedures and as scientists seek embryonic stem cells for research.

In 1965 the bishops of the Second Vatican Council included abortion in a list of offenses against life as they highlighted the importance of respect for life (GS 27). They also referred to it as a crime like infanticide as they reflected on marriage and the family as a problem of special urgency (GS 51). In Paul VI's 1967 encyclical on development, *Populorum Progressio* (On the Development of Peoples), one sees concern about abortion as a means to population control.[52] In Paul VI's 1968 encyclical, *Humanae Vitae* (On the Regulation of Birth), abortion is identi-fied as an immoral way to regulate the size of one's family.[53] As laws changed to allow abortion, the Congregation for the Doctrine of the Faith issued a declaration on abortion in 1974 that reflected the Catholic tradition's natural law method of reasoning.[54] A little over twenty years later, at the request of the College of Cardinals, John Paul II wrote about abortion as contrary to the Gospel. This teaching was more attentive to the sinful structures that contribute to abortion (EV 59). Not only did John Paul II appeal to the principle of no direct tak-ing of innocent human life, but he also appealed to Scripture and other writings from the tradition (EV 61). The former declaration is an appeal to the use of reason to conclude that abortion is an intrinsic evil. This deontological approach faces challenges from a consequentialist ethic, among others. John Paul II's latter appeal draws more explicitly on the faith tradi-tion to indicate that the ordinary universal magisterium has taught infallibly about abortion (EV 62).

Sexual Revolution and Catholic Teaching

In the 1960s there were movements to control birth not only through abortion but also through contraception. From the birth control pill to condoms to sterilization, people sought ways to prevent conception both within marriage and outside of marriage. Movements formed to increase access to and use of contraceptives. In some cases this meant changing laws that restricted access to them. In other cases it meant overcoming financial obstacles to obtaining contraceptives. In still other cases it meant overcoming barriers to effectively using them. Societal values about sexuality in some Western countries were very different from those expressed in church teaching.

During the 1960s the papal birth control commission met to advise the pope on whether church teaching prohibiting the use of contraceptives should change to allow their use within marriage. While the Second Vatican Council named marriage and the family as a topic of special urgency, it could not address the issue of contraception. Paul VI had reserved that question to himself. Three years after *Gaudium et Spes*, Paul VI issued *Humanae Vitae*. In the midst of the sexual revolution, this encyclical reflected both development in teaching about marriage and continuity in teaching about the use of artificial contraception. In an era of ecumenism, it maintained a contrast with the earlier Anglican change in teaching that had prompted the promulgation of *Casti Connubii* (On Christian Marriage) in 1930.[55] *Humanae Vitae* insisted that the physical expression of marital love always be open to the transmission of life (HV 1).

The magisterium's teaching about the unitive and procreative ends of marriage in *Humanae Vitae* is at the core of the conclusions it has reached regarding not only contraception but also assisted reproductive technologies and homosexual marriage. Contraception separates sexual intercourse and procreation for the sake of avoiding births. Assisted reproductive technologies (at least those which the magisterium finds morally problematic) separate sexual intercourse and procreation for the sake of conceiving a child. In the case of homosexual marriage, the physical expression of love is not open to the possibility of creating a new human being. Catholic teaching identifies all three as intrinsically disordered expressions of love.[56]

Not only is Catholic teaching about procreation countercultural in many Western societies but so too is its understanding of the permanence of marriage. In societies with high rates of divorce, the Catholic Church's teaching about the indissolubility of marriage stands in stark contrast with societal practices. Because of this understanding of the indissolubility of marriage, Catholics who are divorced are not allowed to remarry, and those who seek an annulment for a prior marriage receive a judgment about whether a valid marriage existed in the first place.[57] At times, these teachings and practices are experienced as obstacles to faith. At the same time, they are upheld to avoid obstacles to faith.

Scandal in the Midst of Change

Social movements advocating change invite the identification of scandal from a sociological perspective. They identify a situation as wrong. They protest against it in various forms, and they try to raise public interest in that particular issue. The dynamics of sociological scandal function as a strategy for social change in cultural values and laws.

When the Catholic Church takes social movements seriously as signs of the times and evaluates them in light of the Gospel, these movements at times help the Catholic Church deepen its commitment to the Gospel. For example, theological reflection on liberation movements in Latin America deepened the church's concern for the poor by calling for a preferential option for the poor. At other times these movements motivate the church to challenge the changes in policies and social structures that are contrary to human flourishing. This has been the case in response to the sexual revolution and the death with dignity movement. At still other times, the movements call the church to conversion. For example, social movements have challenged the church to move away from racist and sexist practices. In the midst of societal change and concerned about change in Catholic teaching, some Catholics turn to the language of scandal.

Identifying Scandal

When Catholics resort to public denunciation of scandal, it raises the question of the criteria by which they identify scandal. If they were to use the definition of scandal from the Catholic moral tradition, described in chapter one, a definitive list would be difficult to develop. Whether intentional or not, whether serious or not, a person's evil action, or even apparently evil action, can lead another to stumble or fall in his or her relationship with God, for sin has social effects. Catholic public discourse about scandal does not use such a broad definition of scandal. Some who appeal to the language of scandal are doing so based on references to scandal in canon law, but the Code of Canon Law does not define the term.[58]

Positions judged to be dissent from Catholic teaching about abortion, euthanasia, reproductive technologies, contraception, homosexuality, and women's ordination are the ones most frequently labeled scandalous, at least by US Catholics inclined to use this language. At first glance, it might appear that all of the positions pertain to sexuality, but euthanasia is also part of the list. At first glance, it might appear that all of the positions pertain to life, but women's ordination is also part of the list. At first glance, it might appear that all of the positions involve moral issues judged "intrinsically evil" or "intrinsically disordered," but women's ordination is not described with these terms from the Catholic moral tradition. It is also worth noting that this language tells not the seriousness of the evil but rather the constancy of the judgment. At first glance, it might appear that all of the positions have been taught infallibly. Since neither popes nor councils have defined these teachings, that presumes an assessment about the teaching of the ordinary universal magisterium. Only in the cases of abortion, euthanasia, and women's ordination did John Paul II declare his assessment, and statements by bishops call the last assessment into question. Sexuality, life, intrinsic evil (or disorder), and infallibility, either alone or in combination, are not the decisive factors in identifying scandal, though the convergence of these factors sheds light on the centrality of abortion in discourse about scandal.

Underlying these judgments about scandal is a theology of God's dominion. This theology emphasizes that God is the one to give life through the gift of human sexuality, and human sexuality is to serve this end. Human beings are not to destroy human life, because it belongs to God; however, for the sake of the common good, God has delegated authority over life to the state when war and capital punishment are necessary. This theology, found in the moral manuals before the Second Vatican Council, emphasizes the authority of God the Creator who is Lord. A similar appeal to the authority of God, this time expressed through Christ the Lord, appears in arguments against women's ordination. Magisterial teaching against the ordination of women appeals to the will of Christ as expressed in Jesus' choice of twelve male apostles. The positions most frequently identified as scandalous are ones that a preconciliar theology identifies as contrary to God's dominion and Christ's will.

Commenting on *Evangelium Vitae*, Catholic ethicist James Keenan notes references to both God's dominion and intrinsic human dignity to explain the sacredness of human life.[59] Comparing this writing of John Paul II with the moral manuals leads him to an assessment that John Paul II introduced into Catholic teaching an understanding of the sacredness of human life based on human dignity. If the Second Vatican Council's *Gaudium et Spes* were introduced into the analysis, one might conclude that John Paul II was trying to hold together the preconciliar manualist tradition of teaching about life in terms of God's dominion and the Second Vatican Council's teaching about life in terms of intrinsic human dignity

(GS 27). Those in the church who emphasize continuity with Vatican I would be more inclined to retrieve the category of God's dominion found in the moral manuals, and those that emphasize development with Vatican II would be more inclined to emphasize human dignity, the theme of the first chapter in the first part of *Gaudium et Spes*.

Based on the latter theology, John Paul II spoke out strongly against the death penalty and war. While some might dissent from his prudential judgment because of their political loyalties, others might be influenced by John Paul II's own use of the theology of God's dominion from the manualist tradition. From this perspective, state killing in cases of capital punishment and war would not be contrary to God's dominion, because God delegated responsibility for protecting the common good in this way to the state. This older understanding of the sacredness of human life in this case sits in tension with one that is understood in terms of intrinsic human dignity. In *Evangelium Vitae*, John Paul II appeals to an understanding of human life as sacred both because of God's dominion and because of the intrinsic dignity of human beings (EV 39). The tension between understanding the sacredness of life as intrinsic based on God's creative activity and as extrinsic based on God's dominion could be a stumbling block to faith. However, the tension is not normally named in this way. Since those that emphasize continuity are the ones most likely to appeal to the language of scandal used before the council, the language of scandal is more commonly used in relationship to threats to the life of the innocent as well as to sexuality because such actions are judged contrary to God's dominion.

Public Dissent and Scandal

Much of the theological reflection on scandal since the Second Vatican Council has resulted from the hierarchy's concern that public dissent will cause scandal. The widespread nonreception of *Humanae Vitae*'s prohibition of artificial contraception motivated much of this concern. Responding to this, Richard McCormick analyzes the Congregation for the Doctrine of the Faith's 1983 letter to Charles Curran regarding his dissent from magisterial teaching on particular issues of sexual ethics. Because of the letter's concern that public dissent would cause scandal to the faithful, McCormick asks whether "intolerance of any dissent" is "a greater cause of scandal" to the faithful.[60] In a similar fashion, Charles Curran observes, "There has been an unfortunate tendency in the church to exaggerate the scandal of the weak and not to give enough importance to what might be called the scandal of the strong."[61] McCormick and Curran call into question the adequacy of focusing exclusively on avoiding the scandal of the weak, since actions taken toward this end might be a source of scandal to others.

The year after the Congregation for the Doctrine of the Faith's letter to Curran, a *New York Times* advertisement indicated that there was a diversity of views about abortion within the Catholic community. This advertisement provided support to a pro-choice Catholic vice presidential nominee in the United States, Geraldine Ferraro. This responded to Cardinal John O'Connor's affirmative response to a reporter's question about whether such a Catholic should be excommunicated. The hierarchy expressed concern that this advertisement signed by Catholic leaders such as priests, vowed religious, and theologians would cause confusion and lead to scandal.[62] The Vatican applied pressure on some of those who signed the advertisement. Among those who signed the advertisement was Margaret Farley. Reflecting on the Catholic Church's witness in public life more than a decade and a half later, she identified two sources leading to the "scandal of compromised credibility" for the Catholic Church in public life: an "overwhelming preoccupation" with abortion in public life and a repression of thought and discourse within the church.[63]

Catholic leaders' concerns about misinterpretation and confusion are not new, but recent changes have led to greater opportunities for this. If the leaders of the Catholic Church worried about inaccurate interpretation of Scripture at the time of the Protestant Reformation as the printing press made Scripture more accessible to the faithful, they now face a church and world with even greater access to multiple translations of Scripture on the World Wide Web. As the Vatican posts many magisterial documents on the World Wide Web, and as electronic resources make theologians' scholarly articles from journals available on the Web, the hierarchy and theologians face the challenge that other professions face as well. Individuals who are not trained to read technical documents in light of a specialized body of knowledge are doing so. Just as patients can mistakenly arrive at erroneous conclusions based on medical information on the Web, and just as potential clients can arrive at mistaken judgments about the law by reading a specific piece of legislation on the Web, so too can those untrained in a faith community's theological discourse. When people write for one audience and another reads it, this can lead to confusion because of a lack of knowledge. The question of how to negotiate this can be challenging. In these changing times, the need for rich theological discourse is imperative, and at the same time the hierarchy's fear of confusion often results in actions that stifle it.

As a clerical culture that values loyalty and secrecy interacts with an academic culture that values critical reasoning and with democratic cultures that value transparency, conflicts among values are sure to arise. These tensions can undermine trust and raise concerns about the attitude of the other. Such a concern about attitude as a source of scandal appears in the *Catechism of the Catholic Church* after more than a quarter century of tensions regarding the implementation of Vatican II (CCC 2284). In the midst of these tensions, all Catholics are called to witness the Gospel values as central to one's life. Shifting the focus from the vice of scandal to the virtue of charity would reorient the community as it navigates change.

The Catholic Church in Public Life and the Politics of Scandal

CHAPTER 5

In the midst of change in the twenty-first century, Catholics at times struggle to recognize each other in a common profession of faith. While Catholics profess their faith at Mass together on Sundays by reciting the Nicene-Constantinopolitan Creed, they differ in their understanding of what it means to live their faith in public life. One of the areas of life in which this is most evident is in political life, in one's work to promote the common good of the city, the nation, and the global community. To live the Gospel call to proclaim Good News to the poor and marginalized, some stress works of mercy, and others stress changing unjust social structures. To live the Gospel call to promote peace, some, as pacifists, renounce the use of force, and others see a place for it in promoting the common good, among nations in the case of war and within nations in the case of capital punishment. To live the biblical call to choose life, some stress the need to change laws, and others stress the need to change culture. These differences can reflect both different interpretations of revelation and different prudential judgments about its meaning in our world today. The faith community is invited to unity in the midst of this diversity with attention to the way in which the Spirit is at work in these tensions. The prophetic and public approaches to social engagement, which social ethicist Kristin Heyer identifies so well, often offer complementary gifts to the church and world.[1]

As social movements work to change laws and public policies, at times this leads to development in public policies that reflects values in Catholic teaching to a greater degree, such as in the case of the Solidarity movement in Poland in the 1980s.[2] At other times this leads to development in Catholic teaching, such as in the case of the pacifist movement influencing Catholic teaching about war. Not only can changing policies lead to a deeper appropriation of Gospel values, but they can also lead to new conflicts between public policies and the values embodied in the teaching of a faith community. Such has been the case as laws regarding marriage, contraception, abortion, and euthanasia have become more liberal in different countries to varying degrees. This experience of discontinuity between new cultural values and Gospel values shaped the countercultural witness John Paul II called for in *Evangelium Vitae* (On the Value and Inviolability of Human Life). This vision stands in contrast to the dialogical, collaborative approach in *Gaudium et Spes* (Pastoral Constitution on the Church in the Modern World).

The Second Vatican Council encouraged greater participation in the life of one's political community. From Poland to the Philippines, Catholics were major players in peaceful revolutions that toppled dictators in the 1980s. In democracies, Catholics were encouraged to participate in the political process. For instance, in the United States the bishops' conference noted a decline in voter participation in the decade after the Second Vatican Council, and in 1976 they began a quadrennial tradition of issuing statements on political responsibility prior to presidential elections.[3] These statements, addressed to Catholics and non-Catholics alike, invite reflection on making choices that promote human dignity and the common good. In addition to this resource from the national episcopal conference, state episcopal conferences in the United States evaluate proposed legislation and provide resources for lobbying purposes. In 2002 the Congregation for the Doctrine of the Faith reaffirmed the importance of Catholic participation in political life.[4]

Catholics serving the political community as elected or appointed officials at times experience a conflict of conscience regarding voting for legislation or implementing public policy. Laws that are passed can also lead to a conflict of conscience for others when it comes to paying taxes, offering employee benefits, or performing job responsibilities (for instance, in health care, scientific research, or the military). For Catholic educational, health-care, and social service institutions, these laws might call for actions contrary to values articulated in their respective missions. In light of all this, the *Catechism of the Catholic Church* identifies laws and institutions as sources of scandal.[5]

Catholic Institutions, Abortion Laws, and Avoiding Scandal in Germany

Just as the *Catechism of the Catholic Church* was identifying laws and institutions as sources of scandal, the Catholic Church in Germany was facing legal developments that would eventually cause Catholic institutions to reflect on whether their activity was a source of scandal. Following the fall of the Berlin Wall and the reunification of Germany, differences in laws between East Germany and West Germany needed to be reconciled. One legal divide that needed to be bridged was public policy regarding abortion. In East Germany, abortion was allowed for any reason during the first trimester; after that, a medical commission could grant permission if pregnancy threatened a woman's life or if there was another serious reason.[6] In contrast, in West Germany the Constitutional Court held that the constitution provided protection for human life from implantation. This constitutional protection reflected concerns about actions contrary to life performed by the Nazis.[7] While abortion was unconstitutional in West Germany, its law did not penalize those involved in an abortion under certain circumstances.[8]

In 1995, the same year that Pope John Paul II issued the encyclical *Evangelium Vitae,* speaking against sinful structures supporting abortion, Germany formulated its abortion law. This law requires, among other things, that those seeking an abortion obtain a certificate indicating that they have received counseling telling them of the social supports available for a pregnant woman. In the years after this change in law, many Catholic social service agencies, like other religious and state social service agencies, issued these certificates to women they counseled about the social supports available to them. All but one diocese in Germany developed this policy. In January 1998, John Paul II wrote a letter to the German bishops' conference requesting that, in order to avoid scandal, they not issue certificates of counseling.[9] This story made the cover of *Der Spiegel*, including an image associating John Paul II with the crucifixion of women.[10] The bishops' conference formed a working group, which over the course of a year developed a proposal for more assistance, as well as new language for the certificates. Concerned that this could still be used to obtain an abortion, John Paul II required the sentence "This certificate cannot be used to obtain a non-punishable abortion."[11] Eventually, all but one of the bishops complied with Pope John Paul II's judgment to stop issuing certificates, and a year later the one that did not comply was relieved of that particular responsibility.

The German bishops and the pope had arrived at different prudential judgments regarding whether the practice of issuing certificates of counseling would be a source of scandal and whether this was a legitimate form of material cooperation. From John Paul II's perspective, this was immediate material cooperation because the certificate was a necessary condition for an abortion. From the perspective of virtually all of the German bishops, this had been remote material cooperation in which refraining from issuing the certificates (that did not condone abortion) was not sufficient to prevent an abortion, since the state and other religious organizations issued the majority of certificates. The bishops considered such remote material cooperation warranted because it provided the opportunity for life-saving solidarity with women considering abortion. John

Paul II insisted that this was a source of scandal. His effort to avoid this scandal in turn resulted in scandal.

The Vatican's actions certainly generated scandal in the sociological sense. The decision not to issue certificates of counseling violated social expectations and renewed negative orientations dating back to Bismarck's cultural struggle with the Vatican in the nineteenth century. *Der Spiegel* announced this on the magazine's cover.

The Vatican's efforts to avoid scandal also became a source of scandal in the theological sense. The Vatican did not want Catholic teaching about abortion to be undermined through cooperation with the legal system. The decision not to issue certificates that might be used in the process of obtaining an abortion signaled a practical withdrawal of solidarity with pregnant women struggling with the question of how to carry a pregnancy to term. This lack of solidarity was an obstacle to the Catholic Church's witness of God's unconditional love.

Political Participation and the Scandal of Laws: A Look at the 2004 Communion Controversy in the United States

As the church has engaged in its mission by reading the signs of the times in light of the Gospel, the injustice of new laws allowing, and even financially supporting, abortion and euthanasia has made Catholic bishops more aware of laws as a source of scandal. The Congregation for the Doctrine of the Faith, echoing *Evangelium Vitae* in its 2002 Doctrinal Note on Some Questions Regarding the Participation of Catholics in Political Life, states: "John Paul II, continuing the constant teaching of the Church, has reiterated many times that those who are directly involved in lawmaking bodies have a *'grave and clear obligation to oppose'* any law that attacks human life. For them, as for every Catholic, it is impossible to promote such laws or to vote for them."[12] When Catholic legislators resort to the language of "personally opposed but . . . ," it suggests that a pluralistic democracy requires moral relativism rather than reasoned arguments about the justice of particular laws.

Concerned about scandal caused from Catholic politicians voting to support abortion laws, Bishop Raymond Burke issued a statement in his Diocese of LaCrosse, Wisconsin (just months before being transferred to be the archbishop of St. Louis), indicating "that public cooperation in a gravely sinful act, which has always excluded one from worthy reception of the sacrament and is the cause of scandal, was present in the situation."[13] Burke's 2003 statement directed to politicians in his diocese was his attempt at a pastoral embodiment of the Congregation for the Doctrine of the Faith's 2002 doctrinal note. While the statement was directed to the internal life of the church in his diocese, it received national attention as a pro-choice Catholic politician ran for president. It raised the question of whether John Kerry would be denied Communion if he were to present himself for Communion while campaigning in the Archdiocese of St. Louis.

While the cases of public scandal in the moral manuals used in seminaries before the Second Vatican Council did not focus on politicians and laws, John McHugh, OP, and Charles Callan, OP, did consider whether Communion could be administered in cases of public scandal. They state: "If the obligation of reparation is grave, it is not lawful as a rule to admit to [Communion], until the reparation has been actually performed. Thus if it is notorious in a parish that a certain individual has been living in a serious occasion of sin or has been circulating impious doctrines, the occasion of sin should be removed or the doctrines should be retracted, before the individual is admitted to Communion, etc.; otherwise, a new scandal would be given the faithful from the apparent approval given the scandalizer by the minister of the Sacrament received."[14] Burke applied this manualist approach in an effort to avoid scandal from either the politician or the minister of the Eucharist.[15] This approach to avoiding scandal was a source of scandal to others.

The vast majority of US Catholic bishops who responded in a consultation did not share Burke's position with regard to denying Communion. The USCCB's Task Force on Catholic Bishops and Catholic Politicians, which was formed in response to the 2002 doctrinal note, issued an interim report indicating that 75 percent of the bishops who responded in the consultation opposed denying Communion to pro-choice Catholic politicians.[16] In this report, using *Evangelium Vitae*'s declaration that Catholic teachings on abortion and euthanasia are definitive doctrine, Archbishop William Levada indicated that not accepting these teachings diminishes one's "full communion with the faith and life of the church" but does not necessarily prevent one from receiving the Eucharist.[17] At the 2005 Synod on the Eucharist, the US bishops had the opportunity to reflect with other bishops of the world on whether politicians supporting unjust laws could receive Communion. The Synod of Bishops offered the following proposition:

> Catholic politicians and lawmakers must feel their consciences particularly aroused . . . by the heavy social responsibility of presenting and supporting iniquitous laws. There is no Eucharistic coherence when legislation is promoted that goes against the integral good of mankind, against justice and natural law. The private sphere and the public sphere cannot be separated, placing oneself in a position of contrast with the law of God and the teaching of the church, and this must also be considered in Eucharistic terms. In applying this guidance, bishops should exercise the virtues of courage and wisdom, bearing in mind actual local situations.[18]

This language of coherence echoes the doctrinal note on Catholic participation in political life, which indicated the need to be morally coherent and referred to the coherence between faith and life.[19] The Synod of Bishops developed this language of coherence in relationship to the Eucharist. The language of no eucharistic coherence, as opposed to Levada's earlier language of diminished communion, does not admit of degrees and serves as the basis for the USCCB's conclusion that those who lack adherence to definitive moral teaching should not receive Communion.[20]

Some have viewed the denial of Communion in the United
States as politically motivated; however, this is not necessarily the case. Because of the history in the United States of the
Democratic Party adopting a pro-choice position in its party
platform and the Republican Party adopting a pro-life position
in its platform, the likelihood of a pro-choice politician being
a member of the Democratic Party is higher than of one being
a member of the Republican Party. Both parties have a history
of controlling dissenting voices from addressing the respective
plank in each platform. In the 1990s the Democrats would not
allow Governor Bob Casey to speak at the national convention
because he was pro-life, and the Republicans restricted Governor William Weld to speaking about economics at their national
convention since he was pro-choice.[21] It is worth noting that
Archbishop Raymond Burke, the leading spokesperson favoring
denial of Communion, was consistent in his assessment across
parties. His position was equally applicable to John Kerry as he
campaigned to be the Democratic Party's presidential nominee
in 2004 and to Rudolph Giuliani as he campaigned to be the
Republican Party's presidential nominee in 2008.

Burke's bipartisan approach to denying Communion was
rooted in his interpretation of canon law as calling for this
penalty in response to an individual causing serious scandal.
Other canonists such as John Beal have disagreed with his
interpretation of canon law.[22] For many, the denial of Communion is scandalous because of the way in which it is contrary
to Jesus' inclusive table fellowship in the gospels.

During 2004 the Communion controversy was not limited to
politicians but extended to other Catholic citizens engaged in
political life. Some bishops, such as Bishop Michael Sheridan
of Colorado Springs, wrote that if a Catholic voted for a politician whose policies on abortion, euthanasia, embryonic stem
cell research, cloning, and homosexual marriage would conflict
with Catholic teaching on these issues, that person could not
receive Communion prior to confessing cooperation in this
evil.[23] Offering a corrective to this perspective, then-Cardinal

Joseph Ratzinger as head of the Congregation for the Doctrine of the Faith wrote to the US Catholic bishops, recalling the Catholic tradition's teaching about remote material cooperation for their discernment about the relationship between Catholic participation in political life and the Eucharist.[24]

An Honorary Degree from a Catholic University: A Question of Scandal

Just as Catholics in the United States think of John Kerry when they hear "Communion controversy," they think of Barack Obama when they hear "commencement controversy." In anticipation of the president of the United States addressing the 2009 graduating class at the University of Notre Dame, Catholics debated whether he should be the commencement speaker and receive an honorary degree, given his pro-choice stance. The concern was one of a Catholic institution being a source of scandal and betraying its Catholic identity.

The University of Notre Dame has a history of each president of the United States, since Eisenhower, being a commencement speaker. This was not viewed as an affirmation of an individual president's policies but as a symbol of dedication to country. In 2004 the United States Conference of Catholic Bishops issued a prudential judgment indicating that Catholic institutions should not give honors or platforms to individuals holding positions contrary to Catholic teaching.[25] The institution decided to pursue a different course of action to avoid scandal. They chose to honor Mary Ann Glendon with the university's highest award for embodying Catholic values, the Laetare Medal. Glendon is a well-known pro-life advocate who represented the Vatican at the United Nations' Fourth World Conference on Women in 1995. In the midst of the public controversy about Obama as commencement speaker, she chose not to receive the award. Another well-known pro-life Catholic scholar, John Noonan, who was a past recipient of the award, spoke in her place.[26]

This was not the first time or only issue for which protests of commencement speakers at Catholic schools occurred. In fact, Notre Dame's 2006 commencement speaker was a Catholic pro-life politician serving as the president of Ireland, and a lay Catholic group objected because of her position on women's ordination.[27] When speakers' views have conflicted with Catholic teaching about abortion, contraception, embryonic stem cell research, homosexual marriage, and women's ordination, some lay Catholic organizations have indicated that the Catholic institution was a source of scandal. Some have questioned the reduction of Catholic teaching to such a short list. Motivated by others' inattention to important matters in Catholic social teaching, faculty at Boston College also protested a commencement speaker as contrary to the institution's Catholic identity, but they did not turn to the language of scandal in their letter of protest.

When Boston College announced that it would give Secretary of State Condoleezza Rice an honorary law degree as the 2006 commencement speaker, social ethicists David Hollenbach and Kenneth Himes wrote a letter expressing strong disagreement with the Boston College administration's decision. More than two hundred members of the Boston College faculty signed the letter.[28] The letter states, "On the levels of both moral principle and practical moral judgment, Secretary Rice's approach to international affairs is in fundamental conflict with Boston College's commitment to the values of the Catholic and Jesuit traditions and is inconsistent with the humanistic values that inspire the university's work."[29] The letter argues that at the level of moral principle her understanding of national self-interest as the basis of US foreign policy is in conflict with Catholic teaching about solidarity and the global common good. The letter also argues that at the level of practical moral judgment the strategy for the war in Iraq, which she helped develop and implement, does not embody the values of Catholic teaching about just war, both in terms of *ad bellum* ([going] to war) and *in bello* (in war).

The Congregation for the Doctrine of the Faith's doctrinal note invites reflection on institutional embodiment of Catholic identity, as it observes, "In recent years, there have been cases within some organizations founded on Catholic principles, in which support has been given to political forces or movements with positions contrary to the moral and social teaching of the Church on fundamental ethical questions."[30] Encouraged by this, organizations like the Cardinal Newman Society have identified commencement speakers that compromise a Catholic educational institution's identity and cause scandal. If they often identify individuals who in some way compromise the church's teaching about life, sexuality, and women's roles in the church, the Boston College faculty drew attention to social teaching about solidarity and the global common good that often receives less attention.

Catholic Health Care and the Potential for Scandal

As Catholic health-care institutions have responded to the call of the Second Vatican Council to be engaged in the world, they have become more attentive to the possibility that their Catholic identity could be compromised through certain forms of cooperation. Even before the Second Vatican Council, Jesuit moral theologian Gerald Kelly invited Catholic hospitals to consider a way in which the use of technology might lead to scandal for the institution through material cooperation.[31] During the past half century of advances in medical technology and the expenses associated with them, Catholic hospitals have entered into more complex relationships with other health-care providers.[32] While institutional scandal from Catholic hospitals was not a typical case study before the Second Vatican Council, Catholic bishops' concern about institutional scandal from Catholic hospitals has informed their formulation of Ethical and Religious Directives for Catholic Health Care Services.[33]

Representing the United States' largest not-for-profit health-care provider network, the Catholic Health Association was actively engaged in the US health-care reform debate. It worked together with the United States Conference of Catholic Bishops for an abortion-neutral policy preventing additional support for abortion. Shortly before the vote, they differed in their prudential judgments about the means (executive order or law) necessary to provide such protection to the unborn. The Catholic social justice lobby, NETWORK, aligned itself with the Catholic Health Association, gained the support of leaders of women's religious communities, and wrote letters to representatives in Congress advocating for the passage of the bill.[34] In this case some would negatively judge the sisters for not supporting the bishops in their role as public leaders for the Catholic Church, and others would negatively judge the bishops for not supporting sisters engaged in health-care ministry. Not only was there sociological scandal accompanying the positions taken, but there was also concern about theological scandal, which was expressed explicitly by Bishop Thomas Tobin, who insisted that a hospital in his diocese withdraw from the Catholic Health Association.[35]

Shortly after this story, there was another story involving conflict between a religious sister and a bishop. A few months before the passage of the health-care reform bill, a pregnant woman with pulmonary hypertension who had chosen not to have an abortion despite her health risks arrived in the emergency room of a Catholic hospital in a situation judged to be fatal. The ethics committee of the hospital judged the removal of the placenta necessary to save her life not to be a direct abortion, and the surgery was performed to save her life. The bishop of the diocese judged this to be a direct abortion and declared that the Mercy sister who was vice president of mission had excommunicated herself. The hospital did not concur in the bishop's assessment and respond as directed. This failure to respond coupled with previous differences of judgment led the bishop to revoke the hospital's status as Catholic.[36]

Scandal and Religious Liberty

Catholic institutions face challenges to contributing to the church's mission in the world. In the midst of changing cultural values and laws, Catholic institutions in secular countries are facing new requirements at times to act in ways contrary to the institution's values and mission. As conscience clauses are written in narrow terms reflective of a sect model of engagement and focused on worship alone, Catholic institutions face more limited opportunities to carry out their missions with integrity.[37] The spirit of cooperation, collaboration, and dialogical engagement from Vatican II has declined. Where there used to be more focus on God's activity in the world, there is now greater focus on sin in the world. As the world looks at the church, the scandal of sin within the church obscures the proclamation of the Good News. This is the situation in public life that the Catholic Church needs to move beyond.

Conclusion
Beyond Scandal

"Beyond scandal" is a statement of hope. This hope is neither optimism nor wishful thinking. The best public relations campaign is not likely to reorient attitudes toward the Catholic Church, for leaders of the church have both challenged lifestyles based on their understanding of the Gospel and betrayed Gospel values (as well as cultural values in many cases) through their use of power, financial resources, and sex. The Holy Spirit, though, can foster repentance and forgiveness in the human heart. While the best confession is unlikely to change a disciple's sinful habits, with God's grace change is possible. Augustine could confess the need to change from vice to virtue, the need for God's grace to have that happen, and the lack of will to ask for the grace to change. Augustine recalls this after he had, in fact, asked for and received the grace to change. While Augustine's experience reminds us that the discontinuity between faith and life is a perennial challenge, it also reminds us that it is not the end of the story.

The best leader, whether in the church or in society, is unlikely to change cultural values or organizational structures to reflect the Gospel completely, for the message of the Gospel challenges a world of disordered relationships that are difficult to bring into right relationship. Certainly, there are actions that individuals and organizations can and should take to avoid scandal, but avoiding scandal is not absolute from the perspective of the Gospel. It is with good reason that discussions of scandal were traditionally situated in relationship to charity, or friendship with God, and more recently situated in relationship to the biblical command to love one's neighbor.

One can expect that proclamation of God's reign will result in scandal just as it did when Jesus proclaimed it. This proclamation of God's reign led to the cross, but it did not end with the cross. The experience of God's love being stronger than sin and death provides a foundation for hope. God's love brings new life in unexpected places.

The faithful witness of disciples nurtures the gift of hope. It was unlikely that an old pope chosen for the sake of a short pontificate would call a council that would reform the Catholic Church's self-understanding through liturgy, ecumenism, interreligious dialogue, more participation in the life of the church, and engagement in the life of the world. It was unlikely that an anarchist living the sexually permissive lifestyle of the Roaring Twenties would choose to leave her common-law marriage to become a Catholic and would found the Catholic Worker Movement and be a strong Catholic pacifist. It was unlikely that a Catholic sister from a teaching order in Europe would found a religious order to serve the poorest of the poor in India and be an outspoken advocate for life to the world's political leaders. It was unlikely that a boy from a poor, single-parent home in South Carolina would become arguably the most influential implementer of Vatican II in the US Catholic Church as well as the cardinal archbishop of Chicago. It was unlikely that a reluctant bishop, who did not support the way Vatican II was being implemented in his country, would make a preferential option for the poor that would challenge the government of El Salvador, leading to his assassination while saying Mass. It was unlikely that the College of Cardinals would select a Polish pope and that he would play such an influential role in the demise of the Warsaw Pact. Looking more to the moments when people chose to cooperate with God and their actions bore great fruit than to the moments when people failed in ways both large and small can foster the growth of the gift of hope. The Catholic Church as a community of disciples desiring to move beyond scandal would do well to turn to the gospels.

Jesus often told parables about grace, about the experience of the reign of God entering people's lives. These stories were often disorienting for the audience and invited them to look at the world differently. Not only did these stories tell people about God's grace, but the very presence of the storyteller also communicated God's grace. Entering into gospel accounts about Jesus can free Catholic moral imaginations and enable Catholics to respond more faithfully as a community of disciples in our world today. Jesus' interactions with the Samaritan woman at the well and with Peter challenge contemporary Catholic discourse about scandal.

Jesus and the Samaritan Woman at the Well

The Gospel of John tells of Jesus, who was thirsty from his travel, asking a Samaritan woman at a well for some water to drink. Had Jesus focused on avoiding scandal, he would not have done this. He took the risk of potential negative judgment from being alone with this woman at the well. Not only that, but he did this knowing her history. She had been divorced more times than was allowed both by Jewish law and by the more liberal Samaritan interpretation of the law. In addition to that, she was living with a man she was not married to. Jesus entered into dialogue with her, and she experienced God's grace. She returned to her village to share the Good News with others and many believed because of her witness (John 4:4-30, 39-42).

Peter as Rock of Faith and Stumbling Block

As one listens to the Gospel, one hears of Simon (Peter) faithfully professing Jesus to be the Messiah and of Jesus responding to Simon's faith in the Father's revelation by naming him the rock (Peter) upon which Jesus would build his church (Matt 16:13-19). This "rock," though, becomes a stumbling block for Jesus when Peter tempts him to turn away from the way of the cross (Matt 16:21-23). One also hears Jesus telling his friends the night before he died that their faith would be shaken and Peter boldly insisting that his would not be, even after Jesus predicts that Peter will deny him three times (Matt 26:33-35). One hears that Peter falls asleep three times after Jesus repeatedly asks him to keep watch while Jesus prays in the garden of Gethsemane. Then, after Jesus' arrest, Peter denies Jesus three times (Matt 26:38-45, 69-75). In the final chapter of the Fourth Gospel, one hears Jesus ask Peter three times whether he loves him, Peter respond each time affirmatively, and Jesus commission him to serve (John 21:15-19).

Peter professes faith in Jesus as the Messiah, but he finds the thought of Jesus suffering as a result of proclaiming God's reign to be a scandal. In light of this, he becomes a scandal to Jesus by tempting him to avoid the way of the cross. After Jesus' arrest, Peter fears being associated with Jesus and so denies knowing him. This failure to witness to Jesus as the Messiah illustrates both theological and sociological scandal. After Peter stumbled, Jesus calls forth a threefold profession of love to overcome Peter's threefold denial rooted in fear, according to the Gospel of John. With this love that casts out fear, Peter prepares to respond to the risen Lord's call to follow.

Following Christ

These stories of Jesus' interactions with the Samaritan woman at the well and with Peter model virtues necessary for moving beyond scandal. Jesus did not let fear of scandal limit him in courageously listening to this woman and proclaiming God's reign. He did not avoid, exclude, or silence her because of sin or a different interpretation of God's revelation, but rather he shared the Word of God with the excluded, empowering her to be a minister of the Gospel. The church would do well to return to a greater valuing of dialogue as a means to overcome differences and foster the proclamation of God's reign. Just as there are ecumenical dialogues to reconcile a divided Body of

Christ, there is need for more dialogue, like that sponsored by the Catholic Common Ground Initiative, to reconcile divisions within a Catholic Church divided over the meaning of the Second Vatican Council for the life of the church.

Jesus chose followers, such as Peter, who failed him in many ways, but he called forth from them expressions of faith, love, and service. From a disciple's failures can come growth in the virtues of humility and of dependence on God. Jesus reveals God, who is Mystery, and invites a response of faith. Disciples grow in faith as they attend to Christ's presence in their lives and respond with trust. Through spending time with Christ in prayer, they grow in love both of God and of God's creation. Christ invites his followers to express this love in service that manifests God's reign.

A Church of Faith, Hope, and Love

The church is a community of disciples engaged in this mission of proclaiming God's reign. Proclaiming faith in God incarnate who suffered, died, and is risen from the dead is a scandal to many in both secular and religiously pluralistic societies. Proclaiming and witnessing God's special concern for the poor and marginalized challenges the scandal of poverty and inequality found in both society and the church. A church of faith needs to move beyond a fear of confusion to a lovingly courageous dialogue about the Good News and its significance for our world today.

To speak of a church of hope is a reminder that the theological virtues truly are gifts from God. For the past decade, the Catholic Church has lived Good Friday within the community, knowing that the sins and failures of religious leaders created crosses for innocent victims to carry. Good Friday is the point at which the virtue of hope is both most challenging and most necessary. This experience of Good Friday is a time to pray for those who were abused, those who abused them, and all who have been affected by the abuse, because God can bring new life out of this destructive situation. For many, both within and outside the Catholic Church, their relationship to the church has changed. Many who belong to the church feel a sense of betrayal and anger. Many in public life who looked to the Catholic Church as a source of moral authority have given up on that possibility and are now more focused on the state regulating the activities of Catholic organizations. Aware of both the church's limitedness and the world's needs, the church needs to place its hope in God who can bring new life to the church and the world it is to serve.

Efforts to avoid scandal have resulted in failures of love. Abusive priests were moved to new parishes to avoid scandal but these actions failed to express love for the children and families of the new parish. Catholic social service agencies stopped issuing certificates of counseling in Germany to avoid scandal but this action failed to express an interest in reaching out to and loving those who might consider an abortion. Judgments about fidelity to Catholic teaching are rarely accompanied by loving concern for the person with whom one disagrees. For the Christian, the principle of avoiding scandal should not lead to actions contrary to love of God and neighbor. As the church grows in its capacity to be a community of love, there will be little need to think about the principle of avoiding scandal because love of God and neighbor will lead to the avoidance of this type of scandal.

To the extent that the church is a church of love, it will move beyond the scandal of sin. As it embodies the reign of God, it will challenge the scandal of poverty and injustice. The community of disciples is to read the signs of the times and interpret them in light of the Gospel. There is no doubt that in doing so there is much the Spirit could send the community of disciples to do in order to make God's love more present in our world.

Notes

Preface—pages xi–xiv

[1] On the importance of the disciple's courage to speak, see Donald Cozzens, *Faith That Dares to Speak* (Collegeville, MN: Liturgical Press, 2004), 6–9.

[2] *Catechism of the Catholic Church*, 2nd edition (Washington, DC: United States Conference of Catholic Bishops, 2000), 551, nos. 2284–87.

[3] Second Vatican Council, Declaration on Religious Liberty (*Dignitatis Humanae*), December 7, 1965, in *Vatican Council II: Volume 1, The Conciliar and Post Conciliar Documents*, ed. Austin Flannery, OP, new rev. ed. (Northport, NY: Costello Publishing Company, 1996), 799–812.

[4] Second Vatican Council, Pastoral Constitution on the Church in the Modern World (*Gaudium et Spes*), December 7, 1965, in *Vatican Council II*, ed. Flannery, 903–1001.

[5] This is true not only in relationship to sexual scandals but also in relationship to financial scandals. For some steps taken to prevent sexual abuse scandals, see, e.g., Cardinal Seán O'Mally, OFM Cap, Ten Years Later—Reflections on the Sexual Abuse Crisis in the Archdiocese of Boston, January 4, 2012, http://www.bostoncatholic.org/uploadedFiles/BostonCatholicorg/_Utility/News_And_Press/reflections-on-the-sexual-abuse-crisis-in-the-archdiocese-of-boston01-04-2012.pdf; Publication with Respect to Archdiocesan Clergy Accused of Sexual Abuse of a Child, August 25, 2011, http://www.boston catholic.org/publication.aspx; Cindy Wooden, "Vatican Orders Bishops to Draft Guidelines to Handle Sex Abuse Cases," Catholic News Service, May 16, 2011, http://www.catholicnews.com/data/stories/cns/1101921.htm; and United States Conference of Catholic Bishops, Charter for the Protection of Children and Young People (revised 2011), http://usccb.org/issues-and-action/child-and-youth-protection/upload/Charter-for-the-Protection-of-Children-and-Young-People-revised-2011.pdf. For steps to prevent financial scandals, see Most Rev. Daniel F. Walsh, Chairman, United States Conference of Catholic Bishops' Ad Hoc Committee on Diocesan Audits, Report to the Body of Bishops, November 12, 2007, http://old.usccb.org/finance/Report%20to%20Bishops%20Nov%2007.pdf.

Introduction—pages 1–6

[1] Second Vatican Council, Pastoral Constitution on the Church in the Modern World (*Gaudium et Spes*), December 7, 1965, in *Vatican Council II:*

Volume 1, The Conciliar and Post Conciliar Documents, ed. Austin Flannery, OP, new rev. ed. (Northport, NY: Costello Publishing Company, 1996), 903–1001.

[2] Benedict XVI, Address of His Holiness Benedict XVI on the Occasion of Christmas Greetings to the Roman Curia, December 20, 2010, http://www .vatican.va/holy_father/benedict_xvi/speeches/2010/december/documents/ hf_ben-xvi_spe_20101220_curia-auguri_en.html.

[3] Second Vatican Council, Declaration on Religious Liberty (*Dignitatis Humanae*), December 7, 1965, in *Vatican Council II*, ed. Flannery, 799–812.

[4] Benedict XVI, World Day of Peace Message: Religious Freedom, the Path to Peace, January 1, 2011, nos. 1–3, http://www.vatican.va/holy_father/ benedict_xvi/messages/peace/documents/hf_ben-xvi_mes_20101208_xliv -world-day-peace_en.html.

[5] See, e.g., *Hearing on State of Religious Liberty in the United States, Before the Judiciary Committee of the United States House of Representatives, Subcommittee on the Constitution*, 112th Congress, 8–14 (October 26, 2011) (testimony of Most Reverend William C. Lori, Bishop of Bridgeport, on behalf of the United States Conference of Catholic Bishops), http://judiciary.house.gov/hearings/ printers/112th/112-63_70913.pdf.

[6] When Catholic institutions withdraw from activities because conscience rights are not respected, this is an application of the principle of avoiding scandal. See, e.g., Daniel Cardinal DiNardo, "Preventive Services Letter," September 7, 2011, http://www.usccb.org/issues-and-action/religious -liberty/conscience-protection/upload/preventive-letter-to-house-2011-09 .pdf; and Michelle Boorstein and William Wan, "D.C. Archbishop Defends Catholic Charities' Stand on Health Benefits," *The Washington Post*, March 3, 2010, http://www.washingtonpost.com/wp-dyn/content/article/2010/03/02/ AR2010030203947.html.

[7] While the scandal of abuse is not limited to priests in terms of perpetrators, to minors in terms of victims, or to sexual abuse in terms of substance, it is this configuration that has received the most attention in the media.

[8] Thomas P. Doyle, OP, JCD, and Stephen C. Rubina, Esq., "Catholic Clergy Sexual Abuse Meets the Civil Law," *Fordham Urban Law Journal* 31, no. 2 (January 2004): 549–55. For a brief but thorough overview of developments in the United States by a religious provincial responding during this period, see Joseph P. Chinnici, OFM, *When Values Collide: The Catholic Church, Sexual Abuse, and the Challenges of Leadership* (Maryknoll, NY: Orbis Books, 2010), 15–27. (Such a provincial is comparable to a bishop for religious order priests.) For the perspective of an Australian bishop responding during this period, see Geoffrey Robinson, *Confronting Power and Sex in the Catholic Church: Reclaiming the Spirit of Jesus* (Mulgrave, Victoria: John Garratt Publishing, 2007), 7–23. For the perspective of an Irish bishop, see Colm O'Reilly, "The Dilemma of those in Authority," in *The Church and Child Sexual Abuse: Towards a Pastoral Response*, ed. Eamonn Conway, Eugene Duffy, and Attracta Shields, 61–66 (Blackrock, Co Dublin: The Columba Press, 1999). For the perspective of an English bishop

who responded during this period, see Archbishop Vincent Nichols, "Hard Lessons in These Scandalous Times," *Priests & People* 17, no. 3 (March 2003): 91–95.

⁹ For more on the media, see Carl M. Cannon, "The Priest Scandal," *American Journalism Review* (May 2002) http://www.ajr.org/article.asp?id=2516; The Pew Forum on Religion and Public Life, "The Pope Meets the Press: Media Coverage of the Clergy Abuse Scandal," June 11, 2010, http://pewforum.org/Christian/Catholic/The-Pope-Meets-the-Press--Media-Coverage-of-the-Clergy-Abuse-Scandal.aspx; and David E. DeCosse, "Freedom of the Press and Catholic Social Thought: Reflections on the Sexual Abuse Scandal in the Catholic Church in the United States," *Theological Studies* 68, no. 4 (December 2007): 865–74.

¹⁰ Cannon, "The Priest Scandal," http://www.ajr.org/article.asp?id=2516.

¹¹ The Investigative Staff of *The Boston Globe*, *Betrayal: The Crisis in the Catholic Church* (Boston: Back Bay Books, 2003). Cf. Jason Berry, *Lead Us Not into Temptation: Catholic Priests and the Sexual Abuse of Children* (Urbana, IL: University of Illinios Press, 2000).

¹² For articles written by theologians prior to the release of the commission's work, see Patrick Hannon, "Child Sexual Abuse: Rules for the Debate," in *An Irish Reader in Moral Theology*, ed. Enda McDonagh and Vincent MacNamara, vol. 2, *Sex, Marriage and the Family*, 358–64 (Blackrock, Co Dublin: The Columba Press, 2011); and Eamonn Conway, "In Service of a Different Kingdom: Child Sexual Abuse and the Response of the Church," in *An Irish Reader in Moral Theology*, vol. 2, 365–74.

¹³ Commission of Investigation, Report into the Catholic Archdiocese of Dublin, July 2009, http://www.inis.gov.ie/en/JELR/Pages/PB09000504. This report is known as the Murphy Report. For more on the Murphy Report, see John Littleton and Eamon Maher, eds., *The Dublin/Murphy Report: A Watershed for Irish Catholicism?* (Blackrock, Co Dublin: The Columba Press, 2010).

¹⁴ The Ryan Report analyzed child abuse in government-funded institutions for children in Ireland, many of which were run by Catholic religious. For an overview of this report, see Executive Summary of the Commission to Inquire into Child Abuse, May 20, 2009, http://www.childabusecommission.ie/rpt/ExecSummary.php. For an analysis, see *Responding to the Ryan Report*, ed. Tony Flannery (Blackrock, Co Dublin: The Columba Press, 2009). For more on sexual abuse at Canisius College, a Jesuit high school in Berlin, see Sven Röbel and Peter Wensierski, "Jesuit Priest Admits Molesting Youth: Germany Shaken by 'Systematic' Abuse at Berlin Catholic School," *Der Spiegel*, February 1, 2010, http://www.spiegel.de/international/germany/0,1518,675331,00.html. See also an interview of Klaus Mertes, SJ, by Holger Stark and Peter Wensierski, "*Spiegel* Interview with Top Jesuit Priest: We Kept Quiet about Sexual Abuse for Too Long," *Der Spiegel*, July 28, 2011, http://www.spiegel.de/international/germany/0,1518,776775,00.html.

¹⁵ See, e.g., "Catholic Church Sex Abuse Scandals around the World," *BBC News Europe*, September 14, 2010, http://www.bbc.co.uk/news/10407559; Sara Miller Llana, "Latin America Confronts Sexual Abuse by Catholic Priests,"

The Christian Science Monitor, April 12, 2010, http://www.csmonitor.com/World/
Americas/2010/0412/Latin-America-confronts-sexual-abuse-by-Catholic
-priests; and Matthew Tostevin, "Africa Also Suffers Sex Abuse by Priests:
Bishop," *Reuters,* April 8, 2010, http://www.reuters.com/article/2010/04/08/
us-pope-abuse-africa-idUSTRE6372E620100408.

[16] See, e.g., David Hollenbach, "Joy and Hope, Grief and Anguish: *Gaudium
et spes* 40 Years Later," *America,* December 5, 2005, 12–14; and *Hearing on
Substitute Senate Bill 17, Before the Ohio House of Representatives Judiciary Committee*
126th General Assembly (January 11, 2006) (testimony of Bishop Thomas J.
Gumbleton), http://www.natcath.org/mainpage/specialdocuments/Gumbleton
ohiostatement.htm.

[17] Robert Mendick, "Rowan Williams Apologises for Claiming Catholic
Church Has Lost 'All Credibility,'" *The Telegraph,* April 3, 2010, http://www
.telegraph.co.uk/news/religion/7550211/Rowan-Williams-apologises-for
-claiming-Catholic-Church-has-lost-all-credibility.html.

[18] Regarding the United States, see Center for Applied Research and the
Apostolate, "Catholic Reactions to the News of Sexual Abuse Cases Involv-
ing Catholic Clergy," Working Paper 8, by Mark M. Grey and Paul M. Perl
(April 2006): 11, 16–17, http://cara.georgetown.edu/CARAServices/FRStats/
CARA%20WorkingPaper8.pdf. In a poll, the majority in the United States
who stopped giving identified this as a reaction to the sexual abuse scandal.
Among those who contributed at a different level, the motivations varied.
Satisfaction with church leadership declined as the media covered the sexual
abuse scandal. Regarding Germany, see Mark Hallam, "More German Catholics Leave Scandal-Plagued Flock," *Deutsche Welle,* December 19, 2010, http://
www.dw.de/dw/article/0,,6357661,00.html.

[19] In the United States, this includes the Archdiocese of Portland, the
Archdiocese of Milwaukee, the Diocese of San Diego, the Diocese of Tuc-
son, the Diocese of Davenport, the Diocese of Spokane, the Diocese of Fair-
banks, and the Diocese of Wilmington. In addition to these dioceses, the
Oregon Province of the Society of Jesus has also declared bankruptcy. See
Tom Roberts, "Milwaukee Eighth Diocese to File for Bankruptcy," *National
Catholic Reporter,* January 5, 2011, http://ncronline.org/news/accountability/
milwaukee-eighth-diocese-file-bankruptcy.

[20] See, e.g., Abraham McLaughlin, "Scandal's Fallout: The New Struggle
of Catholic Schools," *The Christian Science Monitor,* February 26, 2003, http://
www.csmonitor.com/2003/0226/p01s02-ussc.html.

[21] See, e.g., Archbishop Raymond L. Burke (then bishop of La Crosse),
"Catholics and Political Responsibility" *Origins* 33, no. 33 (January 29, 2004):
557, 559–62.

[22] See M. Therese Lysaught, "Moral Analysis of Procedure at Phoenix Hospital," *Origins* 40, no. 33 (January 27, 2011): 537–49; Bishop Thomas Olmsted,
"Phoenix Hospital No Longer Considered Catholic," *Origins* 40, no. 31 (January 13, 2011): 505–7; St. Joseph's Hospital and Medical Center, "Q and A

on Phoenix Hospital's Status," *Origins* 40, no. 31 (January 13, 2011): 507–9; National Catholic Bioethics Center, "Commentary on the Phoenix Hospital Situation," *Origins* 40, no. 33 (January 27, 2011): 549–51; Kevin O'Rourke, "What Happened in Phoenix? The Complicated Reasons behind an Abortion at a Catholic Hospital," *America*, June 21, 2010, http://www.americamagazine .org/content/article.cfm?article_id=12348; Kevin O'Rourke, "Complications: A Catholic Hospital, a Pregnant Mother and a Questionable Excommunication," *America*, August 2–9, 2010, 15–16; and Kevin O'Rourke, "From Intuition to Moral Principle: Examining the Phoenix Case in Light of Church Tradition," *America*, November 15, 2010, 11–14.

[23] See John Paul II, Letter to the Bishops of the German Episcopal Conference, January 11, 1998, http://www.vatican.va/holy_father/john_paul_ii/ letters/1998/documents/hf_jp-ii_let_19980111_bishop-germany_en.html; and Thomas Wenski, "Archbishop Wenski: On Healthcare, Protect 'Rights of Conscience,'" *Miami Herald*, December 2, 2011, http://www.miamiherald .com/2011/12/02/2529212/archbishop-wenski-on-healthcare.html.

[24] The Cardinal Newman Society sponsors NotreDameScandal.com. On this website, one finds a petition that was sent to Notre Dame's president, John Jenkins, CSC, on April 29, 2009. According to the site, more than three hundred thousand people signed the petition. The site also links to public statements by bishops expressing concern about the university's decision in terms of Catholic identity and scandal.

[25] "Tough Crowd! But Seriously, Folks . . ." *South Bend Tribune*, April 23, 2006, http://articles.southbendtribune.com/2006-04-23/news/26930011_1_zeus -students-speaker.

[26] John Coleman, SJ, "Bishop Kevin Dowling: AIDS and Condoms," *In All Things* (blog), *America*, June 9, 2009, http://www.americamagazine.org/blog/ entry.cfm?id=24947991-3048-741E-1288626171072423.

Chapter 1—pages 7–28

[1] See, e.g., Mitchell Landsberg and Henry Chu, "Catholic Abuse Scandal Edges Closer to Pope," *Los Angeles Times*, March 27, 2010, http://articles .latimes.com/2010/mar/27/world/la-fg-priests27-2010mar27; Steve Weatherbe, "Catholic Charities Embroiled in Scandal: 'Unstable' Adoptions on Both Coasts," *National Catholic Register*, December 18, 2005, http://www.ncregister .com/site/article/catholic_charities_embroiled_in_scandal; Laurie Goodstein, "Order Dismisses a Priest Trying to Ordain Women," *The New York Times*, August 8, 2011, http://www.nytimes.com/2011/08/09/us/09priest.html; Mary Kate Cary, "The Gender Conflict in Catholic Church Hierarchy: Priests, Bishops Should Not Dismiss Nuns on Healthcare Reform or Sexual Abuse Scandal," *U.S. News and World Report*, March 31, 2010, http://www.usnews.com/opinion/ articles/2010/03/31/the-gender-conflict-in-catholic-church-hierarchy; "Cardinal Martini's Book Gives Scandal to the Faithful, Archbishop Says," Catholic

News Agency, December 2, 2008, http://www.catholicnewsagency.com/news/ cardinal_martinis_book_gives_scandal_to_the_faithful_archbishop_says; and Barbara Bradley Hagerty, "Nun Excommunicated for Allowing Abortion," National Public Radio, May 19, 2010, http://www.npr.org/templates/story/ story.php?storyId=126985072.

Attentive to such concerns about scandal, Catholic Healthcare East states: "Catholic health care can use adult stem cells because it does not entail destroying nascent human life. Nevertheless, because of popular confusion about the kinds of stem cells, Catholic health care is keeping its distance from all kinds of stem cells to avoid scandal." Catholic Healthcare East, "Stem Cells: New Implications for Catholic Health Care," *Ethics on the Horizon* (October 2010): 1, http://www.che.org/ethics/index.php?id=35.

[2] See, e.g., the controversy over the funeral of Catholic, pro-choice United States senator Edward Kennedy: "Some Reacted Sinfully to Ted Kennedy's Catholic Burial, Bishop Morlino Says," Catholic News Agency , September 6, 2009, http://www.catholicnewsagency.com/news/some_reacted_sinfully_ to_ted_kennedys_catholic_burial_bishop_morlino_says; and Tom McFeely, "O'Malley on Kennedy's Funeral," *National Catholic Register*, September 4, 2009, http://www.ncregister.com/blog/cardinal_omalley_on_kennedys_funeral_mass.

For an example of divisions over Catholic institutional policies and practices, see United States Conference of Catholic Bishops, Fact Sheet on *The Review and Renewal of the Catholic Campaign for Human Development*, http://old .usccb.org/cchd/fact-sheet-cchd-rr-10-2010.pdf.

[3] Ari Adut, *On Scandal: Moral Disturbances in Society, Politics, and Art*, ed. Mark Granovetter, Structural Analysis in the Social Sciences Series (New York: Cambridge University Press, 2008), 11. For more on objectivist and constructivist approaches, see ibid., 8–11.

[4] Ibid., 13–14.

[5] Ibid.

[6] Ibid.

[7] Ibid., 21–22.

[8] Ibid., 24–25.

[9] Ibid., 19.

[10] Ibid., 14–16.

[11] Ibid., 12, 16.

[12] The false accusation of sexual abuse against Cardinal Joseph Bernardin of Chicago serves as a reminder that allegations are not necessarily true. See Joseph Cardinal Bernardin, *The Gift of Peace: Personal Reflections* (New York: Image Books, 1998), 13–41.

[13] For a comparison of "liberal" Catholics' and "conservative" Catholics' interpretations of responsibility for the scandal, see Paul Lakeland, "Understanding the Crisis in the Church," in *Church Ethics and Its Organizational Context: Learning from the Sex Abuse Scandal in the Catholic Church*, ed. Jean M. Bartunek, Mary Ann Hinsdale, and James F. Keenan (Lanham, MD: Rowman & Littlefield Publishers, Inc., 2006), 4–5.

¹⁴ The National Review Board for the Protection of Children and Young People, "A Report on the Crisis in the Catholic Church in the United States," February 27, 2004, IV.B.4, http://old.usccb.org/nrb/nrbstudy/nrbreport.htm; and Commission of Investigation, "Report into the Catholic Archdiocese of Dublin," July 2009, 1.15, 1.30, 1.32, and 1.113; http://www.inis.gov.ie/en/JELR/Pages/PB09000504.

¹⁵ Thomas Aquinas, *Summa Theologica*, complete English edition in five volumes, trans. Fathers of the English Dominican Province (New York: Benziger Brothers, 1948; Allen, TX: Christian Classics, 1981). Hereafter ST.

¹⁶ Fourth Lateran Council, Constitutions, 1215, in *Decrees of the Ecumenical Councils*, vol. 1, ed. Norman P. Tanner, SJ (London: Sheed and Ward, and Washington, DC: Georgetown University Press, 1990), no. 21, "On Confession Being Made, and Not Revealed by the Priest, and on Communicating at Least at Easter," p. 245.

¹⁷ Council of Trent, Decree on Reform, in *Decrees of the Ecumenical Councils*, vol. 2, ed. Norman P. Tanner, SJ (London: Sheed and Ward, and Washington, DC: Georgetown University Press, 1990), canon 18, p. 751.

¹⁸ ST II-II, q. 43, a. 1, *sed contra* and *respondeo.*

¹⁹ St. Jerome, *Commentary on Matthew*, trans. Thomas P. Scheck, The Fathers of the Church, vol. 117 (Washington, DC: The Catholic University of America Press, 2008), 179.

²⁰ ST II-II, q. 43, a. 1, *respondeo.*

²¹ ST II-II, q. 43, a. 1, ad. 5 and reply to obj. 2.

²² See ST II-II, q. 43, a. 1, ad. 1; a. 6, reply to obj. 2; a. 7, ad. 1; a.7, ad. 3; a. 8, reply to obj. 4 for Augustine; and a. 7, *sed contra*, and a. 8, *respondeo* for Gregory.

²³ See, e.g., ST II-II, q. 43, a. 1, reply to obj. 3, and reply to obj. 4.

²⁴ ST II-II, q. 43, a. 3, *sed contra.*

²⁵ ST II-II, q. 43, a. 2, *respondeo.*

²⁶ ST II-II, q. 43, a. 3, *respondeo.*

²⁷ ST II-II, q. 43, a. 1, ad. 2.

²⁸ ST II-II, q. 43, a. 1, reply to obj. 3.

²⁹ ST II-II, q. 43, a. 5, *respondeo.*

³⁰ ST II-II, q. 43, a. 7, *respondeo.*

³¹ For more on the New Testament's use of the term "scandal," see Juan Mateos, "Analisis Semantico de los Lexemas Σκανδαλίζω y Σκάνδαλον," *Filología Neotestamentaria* 2, no. 1 (May 1989): 57–92.

³² ST II-II, q. 43, a. 4, a. 7, and a. 8.

³³ ST II-II, q. 43, a. 1, *respondeo.*

³⁴ Francisco Suarez, SJ, *Opera Omnia: Commentaria in Secundam Secundae Divi Thomae, scilicet, Viginti Quatuor de Fide, Duas de Spe, Tredecium de Charitate Disputationes*, Editio Nova, A. Carolo Berton, 12 (Paris: Apud Ludovicum Vivés, 1858), 720–31.

³⁵ Alphonsus Marie de Liguori, *Theologia Moralis*, Editio Nova, P. Leonard Gaudé, vol. 1 (Rome: Ex Typographia Vaticana, 1905), 336–55.

³⁶ Francis Patrick Kenrick, *Theologiae Moralis*, vol. 2 (Philadelphia: Apud Eugenium Cummiskey, 1842), 318–23. Henry Davis, SJ, *Moral and Pastoral Theology*, vol. 1, 8th ed. (London: Sheed and Ward, 1959), 333.

[37] Fritz Tillmann, *The Master Calls: A Handbook of Morals for the Layman*, trans. Gregory Roettger, OSB (Baltimore, MD: Helicon Press, 1961), 278. Bernard Häring, CSsR, *The Law of Christ: Moral Theology for Priests and Laity*, vol. 2, trans. Edwin C. Kaiser, CPPS (Westminster, MD: The Newman Press, 1963), 473.

[38] Tillmann's intended audience was the laity, and Häring's was the laity and clergy.

[39] "Special care should be given to the perfecting of moral theology. Its scientific presentation should draw more fully on the teaching of holy Scripture and should throw light upon the exalted vocation of the faithful in Christ and their obligation to bring forth fruit in charity for the life of the world." Second Vatican Council, Decree on the Training of Priests (*Optatam Totius*), October 28, 1965, in *Vatican Council II: Volume 1, The Conciliar and Post Conciliar Documents,* ed. Austin Flannery, OP, new rev. ed. (Northport, NY: Costello Publishing Company, 1992), 720.

[40] Cf. Häring, *The Law of Christ*, 478–80; and Second Vatican Council, Pastoral Constitution on the Church in the Modern World (*Gaudium et Spes*), December 7, 1965, in *Vatican Council II*, ed. Flannery, 903–1001, no. 43.

[41] Häring, *The Law of Christ*, 488.

[42] *Catechism of the Catholic Church,* 2nd edition (Washington, DC: United States Conference of Catholic Bishops, 2000), no. 2286.

[43] Second Vatican Council, Decree on Ecumenism (*Unitatis Redintegratio*), November 21, 1964, in *Vatican Council II*, ed. Flannery, 452, no. 1.

[44] Paul VI, *Humanae Vitae* (On the Regulation of Birth), 1968, http://www.vatican.va/holy_father/paul_vi/encyclicals/documents/hf_p-vi_enc_25071968_humanae-vitae_en.html.

See also Charles E. Curran, *Faithful Dissent* (Kansas City, MO: Sheed and Ward, 1986).

[45] *Catechism*, no. 2284.

[46] Cf. ST II-II, q. 43, a. 1, *respondeo*; and *Catechism of the Catholic Church*, no. 2284.

[47] ST II-II, q. 43, a. 1, ad. 1.

[48] *Catechism*, no. 2287.

[49] Ibid., nos. 588–89.

[50] Ibid., no. 591.

[51] Ibid., no. 2284.

[52] Ibid., no. 2269.

[53] Ibid., no. 2285.

[54] Ibid., no. 2286.

[55] See *The Boston Globe*'s "Spotlight Investigation: Abuse in the Catholic Church" (January 2002–April 2004), http://www.boston.com/globe/spotlight/abuse.

[56] John Paul II, Address to the Cardinals of the United States, April 23, 2002, no. 1, http://www.vatican.va/holy_father/john_paul_ii/speeches/2002/april/documents/hf_jp-ii_spe_20020423_usa-cardinals_en.html.

[57] Cardinal Bernard Law's letter can be found here: "Text of Letter from Cardinal Bernard Law to Boston Archdiocese," *The Baltimore Sun*, April 12, 2002, http://www.baltimoresun.com/news/bal-lawletter12,0,4064148.story.

[58] *Catechism*, no. 2389.

[59] As pope, Benedict XVI has taken steps to demonstrate this, meeting with victims both in the United States and in Malta.

[60] *Catechism*, no. 2489.

[61] Ibid., no. 2491.

[62] Ibid., no. 2492.

[63] ST II-II, q. 43, a. 7, *sed contra*.

Chapter 2—pages 29–47

[1] For more on the biblical meaning of "scandal," see Juan Mateos, "Analisis Semantico de los Lexemas Σκανδαλίζω y Σκάνδαλον," *Filología Neotestamentaria* 2, no. 1 (May 1989): 91.

[2] Karl Rahner, *Foundations of Christian Faith: An Introduction to the Idea of Christianity*, trans. William V. Dych (New York: Crossroad, 1982), 116–26.

[3] Michael J. Himes, *Doing the Truth in Love: Conversations about God, Relationships and Service* (Mahwah, NJ: Paulist Press, 1995), 9.

[4] Mary Magdalene was the "apostle of the apostles," John and Peter were two of the Twelve, and Paul was sent by the risen Lord to proclaim the Good News.

[5] Sandra M. Schneiders, IHM, *The Revelatory Text: Interpreting the New Testament as Sacred Scripture*, 2nd ed. (Collegeville, MN: Liturgical Press, 1999), 76–77.

[6] Aaron Milavec, *The Didache: Text, Translation, Analysis, and Commentary* (Collegeville, MN: Liturgical Press, 2003).

[7] The Symbol of the Roman Order of Baptism, in *The Christian Faith in the Doctrinal Documents of the Catholic Church*, ed. J. Neuner, SJ, and J. Dupuis, SJ, 6th rev. and enlarged ed. (New York: Alba House, 1996), 4–5.

[8] Brian E. Daley, SJ, "Structures of Charity: Bishops' Gatherings and the See of Rome in the Early Church," in *Episcopal Conferences: Historical, Canonical, and Theological Studies*, ed. Thomas J. Reese, SJ (Washington, DC: Georgetown University Press, 1989), 25–58.

[9] The Letter of the Synod in Nicaea to the Egyptians, in *Decrees of the Ecumenical Councils*, vol. 1, ed. Norman P. Tanner, SJ (London: Sheed and Ward, and Washington, DC: Georgetown University Press, 1990), 16–17.

[10] The Profession of Faith of the 318 Fathers, in *Decrees of the Ecumenical Councils*, vol. 1, ed. Tanner, 5.

[11] Avery Dulles notes, "The term 'revelation' does not appear in the creeds and is not central in the Scriptures. Treatises on revelation did not begin to be written until the Enlightenment period, in controversies with the Deists." Avery Dulles, SJ, *Models of Revelation* (Maryknoll, NY: Orbis Books, 1992 [1983]), xix.

[12] Pius IX, "Syllabus," or Collection of Modern Errors, in *The Sources of Catholic Dogma*, trans. by Roy J. Deferrari from the 30th ed. of Henry Denzinger's *Enchiridion Symbolorum* (St. Louis, MO: B. Herder Book Co., 1957), 433–42.

¹³ The phrase "and the Son," which is used in Western Christianity to refer to the procession of the Holy Spirit from both the Father and the Son.

¹⁴ Vatican I, Profession of Faith, in *Decrees of the Ecumenical Councils*, vol. 2, ed. Tanner, 802–3.

¹⁵ Vatican I, Dogmatic Constitution on the Catholic Faith, in *Decrees of the Ecumenical Councils*, vol. 2, ed. Tanner, 804–5.

¹⁶ Ibid., pp. 805–6, no. 1.

¹⁷ Ibid., p. 806, no. 2.

¹⁸ Ibid., p. 807, no. 3.

¹⁹ For more on *ressourcement* and development of doctrine, see John W. O'Malley, *What Happened at Vatican II* (Cambridge, MA: The Belknap Press of Harvard University Press, 2008), 36–43.

²⁰ For Murray's argument for development of doctrine regarding religious liberty, see Father John Courtney Murray, "On Development of the Doctrine of Religious Liberty," in *Council Daybook: Vatican II, Session 4, Sept. 14, 1965 to Dec. 8, 1965*, ed. Floyd Anderson (Washington, DC: National Catholic Welfare Conference, 1966), 14–15.

²¹ Rahner, *Foundations of Christian Faith*, 32.

²² Second Vatican Council, Dogmatic Constitution on Divine Revelation (*Dei Verbum*), November 18, 1965, in *Vatican Council II: Volume 1, The Conciliar and Post Conciliar Documents*, ed. Austin Flannery, OP, new rev. ed. (Northport, NY: Costello Publishing Company, 1996), 750–65.

²³ *Council Daybook: Vatican II, Session 4, Sept. 14, 1965 to Dec. 8, 1965*, ed. Anderson, 235.

²⁴ John O'Malley, "Vatican II: Did Anything Happen?" *Theological Studies* 67, no. 1 (March 2006): 3–33.

²⁵ Dulles, *Models of Revelation*, 41–52.

²⁶ See, e.g., Richard A. McCormick, SJ, *The Critical Calling: Reflections on Moral Dilemmas since Vatican II* (Washington, DC: Georgetown University Press, 2006), 121; Charles E. Curran, *Directions in Fundamental Moral Theology* (Notre Dame, IN: University of Notre Dame Press, 1985), 276; Margaret A. Farley, "The Church in the Public Forum: Scandal or Prophetic Witness?" in *The Catholic Church, Morality and Politics*, ed. Charles E. Curran and Leslie Griffin (New York: Paulist Press, 2001), 208; Cathleen Kaveny, "Catholics as Citizens: Today's Ethical Challenges Call for New Moral Thinking," *America*, November 1, 2010, 13–16; Lisa Fullam, "Giving Scandal," *America*, November 1, 2010, http://www.americamagazine.org/content/article.cfm?article_id=12533; and Enda McDonagh, "Scandal," chap. in *Doing the Truth: The Quest of Moral Theology* (Notre Dame, IN: University of Notre Dame Press, 1979), 184–85.

²⁷ The Profession of Faith of Paul VI (1968), in *The Christian Faith in the Doctrinal Documents of the Catholic Church*, ed. Neuner and Dupuis, 24–31.

²⁸ "John Paul II, Congregation for the Doctrine of the Faith, New Formula for the Profession of Faith (9 January 1989)," in *The Christian Faith in the Doctrinal Documents of the Catholic Church*, ed. Neuner and Dupuis, 32.

[29] Ladislas Orsy, SJ, *The Profession of Faith and the Oath of Fidelity: A Theological and Canonical Analysis* (Wilmington, DE: Michael Glazier, 1990), 32.

[30] William Spohn, "The Magisterium and Morality," *Theological Studies* 54, no. 1 (March 1993): 95–111.

[31] Francis A. Sullivan, SJ, *Creative Fidelity: Weighing and Interpreting Documents of the Magisterium* (New York: Paulist Press, 1996), 181. Joseph Ratzinger, "Commentary on the Profession of Faith's Concluding Paragraphs," *Origins* 28, no. 8 (July 16, 1998): 118. For Avery Dulles's position, see the sidebar on p. 117 of Ratzinger's commentary.

[32] John Paul II, *Ordinatio Sacerdotalis* (On Reserving Priestly Ordination to Men Alone), 1994, no. 4, http://www.vatican.va/holy_father/john_paul_ii/apost_letters/documents/hf_jp-ii_apl_22051994_ordinatio-sacerdotalis_en.html.

[33] Sullivan, *Creative Fidelity*, 181–84.

[34] Maureen Fiedler, "The Vatican's Fear of Women," *National Catholic Reporter*, August 11, 2011, http://ncronline.org/blogs/ncr-today/vatican's-fear-women.

[35] John Paul II, *Ad Tuendam Fidem*, May 18, 1998, http://www.vatican.va/holy_father/john_paul_ii/motu_proprio/documents/hf_jp-ii_motu-proprio_30061998_ad-tuendam-fidem_en.html.

[36] See Mother Mary Clare Millea, ASCJ, "Letter to Superiors General Regarding Apostolic Visitation of Women Religious in the United States," May 19, 2009, http://www.apostolicvisitation.org/en/materials/letter_superiors.pdf; and James Martin, SJ, "Apostolic Visitation Update" *In All Things* (blog), *America,* June 15, 2009, http://www.americamagazine.org/blog/entry.cfm?id=56339556-3048-741E-5297111182756936.

[37] Orsy, *The Profession of Faith and the Oath of Fidelity*, 43.

[38] Donald Cozzens, *Sacred Silence: Denial and the Crisis in the Church* (Collegeville, MN: Liturgical Press, 2002), 169.

[39] Cf. The Profession of Faith of the 318 Fathers, in *Decrees of the Ecumenical Councils*, vol. 1, ed. Tanner, 5. The Greek and Latin are found on a page facing the English.

[40] "It will be shed for you and for all so that sins may be forgiven," http://old.usccb.org/romanmissal/samples-priest-prayer4.shtml.

[41] "[W]hich will be poured out for you and for many for the forgiveness of sins," http://old.usccb.org/romanmissal/samples-priest-prayer4.shtml.

[42] Pontifical Council for Justice and Peace, *Compendium of the Social Doctrine of the Church* (Washington, DC: United States Conference of Catholic Bishops, 2004).

[43] *"Since something of the glory of God shines on the face of every person, the dignity of every person before God is the basis of the dignity of man before other men.* Moreover, this is the ultimate foundation of the radical equality and brotherhood among all people, regardless of their race, nation, sex, origin, culture, or class." *Compendium*, no. 144, p. 63.

[44] Response to a question during the question-and-answer session following Cardinal Renato Martino's presentation to the Association of Catholic Colleges and Universities' Catholic Higher Education in a Global Context Seminar, June 16, 2008.

[45] Augustine, *On Christian Doctrine*, trans. D.W. Robertson Jr. (New York: Macmillan, 1958), bk. 1, chap. 6, pp. 10–11.

[46] See Gustavo Gutiérrez, *On Job: God-Talk and the Suffering of the Innocent* (Maryknoll, NY: Orbis Books, 1987), 21–38.

[47] Bradley M. Peper and Mark DelCogliano, "The Pliny and Trajan Correspondence," in *The Historical Jesus in Context*, ed. Amy-Jill Levine, Dale C. Allison Jr., and John Dominic Crossan, Princeton Readings in Religions (Princeton, NJ: Princeton University Press, 2006), 366–71.

[48] Ibid.

[49] Perpetua, "The Martyrdom of Perpetua and Felicitas," in *The Acts of the Christian Martyrs*, trans. Herbert Musurillo (Oxford: Clarendon Press, 1972), 106–31.

[50] Cyprian, *De Lapsis* and *De Ecclesiae Catholicae Unitate*, trans. Maurice Bévenot, SJ, ed. Henry Chadwick, Oxford Early Christian Texts (Oxford: Clarendon Press, 1971), no. 15, pp. 22–23. Maurice Bévenot, "The Sacrament of Penance and St. Cyprian's *De Lapsis*," *Theological Studies* 16, no. 2 (June 1955): 175–213.

[51] For recent analysis of religious persecution, see the United States Department of State, *2010 Report on International Religious Freedom*, http://www.state.gov/g/drl/rls/irf/2010. For a high-profile story of a preferential option for the poor resulting in martyrdom, see James R. Brockman, *Romero: A Life* (Maryknoll, NY: Orbis Books, 1989).

[52] Benedict XVI, World Day of Peace Message: Religious Freedom, the Path to Peace, January 1, 2011, nos. 1–2, http://www.vatican.va/holy_father/benedict_xvi/messages/peace/documents/hf_ben-xvi_mes_20101208_xliv-world-day-peace_en.html.

[53] For a reflection on the significance of this understanding of being a companion of Jesus, see Peter-Hans Kolvenbach, SJ, "The Service of Faith and the Promotion of Justice in Jesuit Higher Education," Santa Clara University, October 6, 2000, http://www.scu.edu/ignatiancenter/events/conferences/archives/justice/upload/f07_kolvenbach_keynote.pdf.

[54] Thomas Aquinas, *Summa Theologica* I-II, q. 90, a. 4, *respondeo*.

Chapter 3—pages 48–65

[1] See, e.g., Tom McFeely, "Harper, Clinton and the Reception of Communion," *National Catholic Register*, July 10, 2009, http://www.ncregister.com/blog/harper_clinton_and_reception_of_communion.

[2] Congregation for the Doctrine of the Faith, Letter to the Bishops of the Catholic Church Concerning the Reception of Holy Communion by the Divorced and Remarried Members of the Faithful, 1994, http://www.vatican.va/roman_curia/congregations/cfaith/documents/rc_con_cfaith_doc_14091994_rec-holy-comm-by-divorced_en.html.

[3] E. J. Dionne Jr., "For an 'Obamacon,' Communion Denied," *The Washington Post*, June 3, 2008, http://www.washingtonpost.com/wp-dyn/content/article/2008/06/02/AR2008060202591.html.

⁴ In the first two cases it was a function of excommunication. See "Religion: The Archbishop Stands Firm," *Time*, April 27, 1962, http://www.time.com/time/ magazine/article/0,9171,896105,00.html; William T. Cavanaugh, *Torture and Eucharist: Theology, Politics and the Body of Christ* (Oxford: Blackwell Publishing, 1998), 253–54; Raymond L. Burke, "Prophecy for Justice: Catholic Politicians and Bishops," *America*, June 21, 2004, 11–15; "Netherlands Gay Protest Over Catholic Communion Snub," BBC News, February 29, 2010, http://news.bbc .co.uk/2/hi/8542285.stm; and John Allen, "Australian Bishops Find Catholic Women Feel Pain, Alienation," *National Catholic Reporter Online*, August 27, 1999, http://natcath.org/NCR_Online/archives2/1999c/082799/082799g.htm.

⁵ Gary Macy, *The Banquet's Wisdom: A Short History of the Theologies of the Lord's Supper* (New York: Paulist Press, 1992), 28–33.

⁶ Ibid., 30–31.

⁷ Klaus Schatz, SJ, *Papal Primacy: From Its Origins to the Present*, trans. John A. Otto and Linda M. Maloney (Collegeville, MN: Liturgical Press, 1996), 4.

⁸ Cyprian, *De Lapsis* and *De Ecclesiae Catholicae Unitate*, trans. Maurice Bévenot, SJ, ed. Henry Chadwick, Oxford Early Christian Texts (Oxford: Clarendon Press, 1971), no. 15, pp. 22–23. Maurice Bévenot, "The Sacrament of Penance and St. Cyprian's *De Lapsis*," *Theological Studies* 16, no. 2 (June 1955): 175–213.

⁹ See Avery Dulles, *Models of the Church* (New York: Image Books, 1991), 8.

¹⁰ First Vatican Council, First Dogmatic Constitution on the Church of Christ (*Pastor Aeternus*), 1870, in *Decrees of the Ecumenical Councils*, vol. 2, ed. Norman P. Tanner, SJ (London: Sheed and Ward, and Washington, DC: Georgetown University Press, 1990), 811–12.

¹¹ Ibid., no. 4.

¹² Schatz, *Papal Primacy*, 167.

¹³ Second Vatican Council, Dogmatic Constitution on the Church (*Lumen Gentium*), November 21, 1963, in *Vatican Council II: Volume 1, The Conciliar and Post Conciliar Documents*, ed. Austin Flannery, OP, new rev. ed. (Northport, NY: Costello Publishing Company, 1996), 350–69, nos. 1–17.

¹⁴ John Paul II, *Apostolos Suos* (On the Theological and Juridical Nature of Episcopal Conferences), 1998, http://www.vatican.va/holy_father/john _paul_ii/motu_proprio/documents/hf_jp-ii_motu-proprio_22071998_apostolos -suos_en.html.

¹⁵ See propositions 42–49 in Synodus Episcoporum Bollettino, XI Coetus Generalis Ordinarius Synodi Episcoporum, 2–23 Octobris 2005, *Eucharista: fons et culmen vitae et missionis Ecclesiae*, http://www.vatican.va/news_services/press/ sinodo/documents/bollettino_21_xi-ordinaria-2005/xx_plurilingue/b31_xx.html.

¹⁶ Ibid., propositions 49, 45, and 47.

¹⁷ John O'Malley, "Vatican II: Did Anything Happen?" *Theological Studies* 67, no. 1 (March 2006): 17–18, 27–30.

¹⁸ For a consideration of the technical distinction between *ressourcement* and development of doctrine, see John W. O'Malley, *What Happened at Vatican II* (Cambridge, MA: The Belknap Press of Harvard University Press, 2008), 36–43.

¹⁹ For more, see John T. Noonan Jr., *A Church That Can and Cannot Change: The Development of Catholic Moral Teaching* (Notre Dame, IN: University of Notre Dame Press, 2005).

²⁰ Benedict XVI, World Day of Peace Message: Religious Freedom, the Path to Peace, January 1, 2011, nos. 1–3, http://www.vatican.va/holy_father/benedict _xvi/messages/peace/documents/hf_ben-xvi_mes_20101208_xliv-world-day -peace_en.html.

²¹ See Paul VI, *Humanae Vitae* (On the Regulation of Birth), 1968, http://www .vatican.va/holy_father/paul_vi/encyclicals/documents/hf_p-vi_enc _25071968_humanae-vitae_en.html.

²² On the death penalty, see John Paul II, *Evangelium Vitae* (On the Value and Inviolability of Human Life), 1995, no. 56, http://www.vatican.va/holy _father/john_paul_ii/encyclicals/documents/hf_jp-ii_enc_25031995 _evangelium-vitae_en.html.

²³ Ratzinger uses papal infallibility as an example of a teaching moving from the category of definitive teaching to that of dogma and suggests that the nonordination of women is undergoing a similar process. See Joseph Ratzinger, "Commentary on the Profession of Faith's Concluding Paragraphs," *Origins* 28, no. 8 (July 16, 1998): 116–19.

²⁴ For more on magisterium, see Francis A. Sullivan, SJ, *Magisterium: Teaching Authority in the Catholic Church* (New York: Paulist Press, 1983).

²⁵ Ratzinger, "Commentary," 116–19.

²⁶ Vatican I, *Pastor Aeternus*, chap. 4.

²⁷ Francis A. Sullivan, SJ, *Creative Fidelity: Weighing and Interpreting Documents of the Magisterium* (New York: Paulist Press, 1996), 82–89.

²⁸ See Richard Gaillardetz, "The Ordinary Universal Magisterium: Unresolved Questions," *Theological Studies* 63, no. 3 (September 2002): 447–71.

²⁹ For more on reception, see Richard Gaillardetz, *Teaching with Authority: A Theology of the Magisterium in the Church* (Collegeville, MN: Liturgical Press, 1997), 227–52.

³⁰ See Cindy Wooden, "Cardinal Levada Says Vatican Preparing New Guidelines to Fight Abuse," Catholic News Service, November 19, 2010, http://www .catholicnews.com/data/stories/cns/1004785.htm; Benedict XVI, Address of His Holiness Benedict XVI on the Occasion of Christmas Greetings to the Roman Curia, December 20, 2010, http://www.vatican.va/holy_father/benedict_xvi/ speeches/2010/december/documents/hf_ben-xvi_spe_20101220_curia-auguri _en.html; and Benedict XVI, Religious Freedom, the Path to Peace, nos. 1–3.

³¹ Benedict XVI, Religious Freedom, the Path to Peace, no. 3

³² Pius IX, "Syllabus," or Collection of Modern Errors, in *The Sources of Catholic Dogma*, trans. by Roy J. Deferrari from the 30th ed. of Henry Denzinger's *Enchiridion Symbolorum* (St. Louis, MO: B. Herder Book Co., 1957), 433–42.

³³ Leslie Griffin, "Commentary on *Dignitatis Humanae* (Declaration on Religious Freedom)," in *Modern Catholic Social Teaching: Commentaries and Interpretations*,

ed. Kenneth R. Himes, OFM (Washington, DC: Georgetown University Press, 2005), 245.

[34] See, e.g., John Courtney Murray, SJ, "Leo XIII: Two Concepts of Government," *Theological Studies* 14, no. 4 (December 1953): 551–67. See also Father John Courtney Murray, "On Development of the Doctrine of Religious Liberty," in *Council Daybook: Vatican II, Session 4, Sept. 14, 1965 to Dec. 8, 1965*, ed. Floyd Anderson (Washington DC: National Catholic Welfare Conference, 1966), 14–15.

[35] John Courtney Murray, *We Hold These Truths* (Kansas City, MO: Sheed and Ward, 1960).

[36] Kevin F. Burke, "Love Will Decide Everything: Pedro Arrupe Recovered the Ignatian 'Mysticism of Open Eyes,'" *America*, November 12, 2007, 21.

[37] For more on the life of Dorothy Day, see Dorothy Day, *The Long Loneliness: The Autobiography of Dorothy Day* (New York: Harper, 1952).

[38] For more on the life of this Nobel Peace Prize recipient, see a biography at http://www.nobelprize.org/nobel_prizes/peace/laureates/1979/teresa-bio .html#.

[39] National Conference of Catholic Bishops, The Challenge of Peace: God's Promise and Our Response, 1983, in *Catholic Social Thought: The Documentary Heritage*, ed. David J. O'Brien and Thomas A. Shannon (Maryknoll, NY: Orbis Books, 1992), 492–571.

[40] Joseph Cardinal Bernardin, *The Gift of Peace: Personal Reflections* (New York: Image Books, 1998), 121–48.

[41] Bartolomé de Las Casas, *The Only Way*, ed. Helen Rand Parish, trans. Francis Patrick Sullivan, SJ (New York: Paulist Press, 1992), 68–74.

[42] Cardinal Joseph Bernardin and Archbishop Oscar H. Lipscomb, *Catholic Common Ground Initiative: Foundational Documents* (New York: The Crossroad Publishing Company, 1997).

[43] Gustav Niebuhr, "Cardinal Opposed in Effort to Find 'Common Ground,'" *The New York Times*, August 24, 1996, http://www.nytimes.com/1996/08/24/us/ cardinal-opposed-in-effort-to-find-common-ground.html.

[44] Barbara Reid, "Having No Enemies," *America*, February 14, 2011, 38.

[45] For more on Romero, see James R. Brockman, *Romero: A Life* (Maryknoll, NY: Orbis Books, 1989).

[46] For more, see Joseph Cardinal Ratzinger, *The Legacy of John Paul II: Images and Memories*, photographs by Giancarlo Giuliani, trans. Michael J. Miller and Nicoletta V. MacKensie (San Francisco: Ignatius Press, 2005), 56–102.

[47] See ibid., 39; and Michael Walsh, "From Karol Wojtyla to John Paul II: Life and Times," in *The Vision of John Paul II: Assessing His Thought and Influence*, ed. Gerard Mannion (Collegeville, MN: Liturgical Press), 22–23.

[48] Ratzinger, *The Legacy of John Paul II*, 104–14

[49] See Bradford E. Hinze, "Placating Polarizations or Making Them Productive?" chap. 5 in *Practices of Dialogue in the Roman Catholic Church: Aims and Obstacles, Lessons and Laments* (New York: Continuum, 2006), 112–29.

[50] John Paul II, *Ut Unum Sint* (On Commitment to Ecumenism), 1995, http://www.vatican.va/holy_father/john_paul_ii/encyclicals/documents/ hf_jp-ii_enc_25051995_ut-unum-sint_en.html.

[51] John Paul II, *Ordinatio Sacerdotalis* (On Reserving Priestly Ordination to Men Alone), 1994, no. 4, http://www.vatican.va/holy_father/john _paul_ii/apost_letters/documents/hf_jp-ii_apl_22051994_ordinatio -sacerdotalis_en.html.

[52] Congregation for Catholic Education, Instruction Concerning the Criteria for the Discernment of Vocations with regard to Persons with Homosexual Tendencies in View of their Admission to the Seminary and to Holy Orders, 2005, http://www.vatican.va/roman_curia/congregations/ccatheduc/documents/ rc_con_ccatheduc_doc_20051104_istruzione_en.html.

Chapter 4—pages 66–84

[1] Second Vatican Council, Pastoral Constitution on the Church in the Modern World (*Gaudium et Spes*), December 7, 1965, in *Vatican Council II: Volume 1, The Conciliar and Post Conciliar Documents*, ed. Austin Flannery, OP, new rev. ed. (Northport, NY: Costello Publishing Company, 1996), 905, no. 4.

[2] For more on the work of poor Christians for liberation, see Curt Cadorette, *From the Heart of the People: The Theology of Gustavo Gutiérrez* (Oak Park, IL: Meyer Stone Books, 1988).

[3] Second General Conference of Latin American Bishops, Peace, in *Renewing the Earth: Catholic Documents on Peace, Justice and Liberation*, ed. David J. O'Brien and Thomas A. Shannon (Garden City, NY: Image Books, 1977), 561–63, nos. 2–7.

[4] See, e.g., Gustavo Gutiérrez, *The God of Life*, trans. Matthew J. O'Connell (Maryknoll, NY: Orbis Books, 1991), xi.

[5] Gustavo Gutiérrez, *A Theology of Liberation: History, Politics and Salvation*, rev. ed., trans. and ed. Sister Caridad Inda and John Eagleson (Maryknoll, NY: Orbis Books, 1988), 162–73.

[6] John Paul II, *Sollicitudo Rei Socialis* (On Social Concern), 1987, in *Catholic Social Thought: The Documentary Heritage*, ed. David J. O'Brien and Thomas A. Shannon (Maryknoll, NY: Orbis Books, 1992), 425, no. 42. Congregation for the Doctrine of the Faith, Instruction on Certain Aspects of the "Theology of Liberation," 1984, chap. 7, "Marxist Analysis," nos. 1–13, http://www.vatican.va/roman_curia/congregations/cfaith/documents/ rc_con_cfaith_doc_19840806_theology-liberation_en.html.

[7] Congregation for the Doctrine of the Faith, Instruction on Certain Aspects of the "Theology of Liberation," nos. 6–9.

[8] "Let us not be guilty of the scandal of having some nations, most of whose citizens bear the name of Christians, enjoying an abundance of riches, while

others lack the necessities of life and are tortured by hunger, disease, and all kinds of misery" (GS 88).

[9] See, e.g., Francis X. Doyle, "For US Bishops, Economic Justice Isn't on the Agenda: Catholic Leaders, Meeting in Baltimore this Week, Fail to Put Society's Main Problems Front and Center," *Baltimore Sun*, November 14, 2011, http://www.baltimoresun.com/news/opinion/oped/bs-ed -bishops-20111111,0,5882195.story.

[10] US Catholic Bishops, Economic Justice for All, in *Catholic Social Thought*, ed. O'Brien and Shannon, 572–680. Pontifical Council for Justice and Peace, Reforming the International Financial and Monetary Systems, *Origins* 41, no. 22 (November 3, 2011): 341–49.

[11] Leo XIII, *Rerum Novarum*, 1891, in *Catholic Social Thought*, ed. O'Brien and Shannon, 14-39.

[12] Bryan N. Massingale, *Racial Justice and the Catholic Church* (Maryknoll, NY: Orbis Books, 2010), 3–5. See also Blasé Cupich, "Racism and the Election," *America*, October 27, 2008, 5.

[13] United States Conference of Catholic Bishops, Forming Consciences for Faithful Citizenship: A Call to Political Responsibility from the Catholic Bishops of the United States, 2007, no. 34, http://www.usccb.org/issues-and-action/ faithful-citizenship/upload/forming-consciences-for-faithful-citizenship.pdf.

[14] Catholic Charities USA, Poverty and Racism: Overlapping Threats to the Common Good, 2008, http://www.catholiccharitiesusa.org/Document .Doc?id=614. See also Bryan N. Massingale, "The Scandal of Poverty: 'Cultured Indifference' and the Option for the Poor Post-Katrina," in "Faithful Citizenship: Principles and Strategies to Serve the Common Good," ed. Dennis Hamm, SJ, and Gail S. Risch, supplement 4, *Journal of Religion and Society* 10 (2008): 55–72, http://moses.creighton.edu/JRS/2008/2008-29.pdf.

[15] See Cyprian Davis, OSB, *The History of Black Catholics in the United States* (New York: Crossroad, 1990), 36–39,197.

[16] See, e.g., ibid., 99, 105, 110, 146, 220.

[17] Administrative Board, National Catholic Welfare Council, Discrimination and the Christian Conscience, November 14, 1958, in *Pastoral Letters of the United States Catholic Bishops*, vol. 2, 1941–1961, ed. Hugh J. Nolan (Washington DC: United States Catholic Conference, 1984), 201–6.

[18] National Conference of Catholic Bishops, Statement on National Race Crisis, April 25, 1968, in *Pastoral Letters of the United States Catholic Bishops*, vol. 3, 1962–1974, ed. Hugh J. Nolan (Washington, DC: United States Conference of Catholic Bishops, 1983), 156–60.

[19] Synod of Bishops, Justice in the World, 1971, in *Catholic Social Thought*, ed. O'Brien and Shannon, 288–300, nos. 42–43.

[20] Ibid., nos. 40-43.

[21] Paul VI, Apostolic Letter on First Tonsure, Minor Orders and the Subdiaconate (*Ministeria Quaedam*), 1972, in *Vatican Council II*, ed. Flannery, 427–32.

[22] Miriam Therese Winter, *Out of the Depths: The Story of Ludmila Javorova, Ordained Roman Catholic Priest* (New York: The Crossroad Publishing Company, 2001), 9–10, 125–28.

[23] Ibid., 183–84; Congregation for the Doctrine of the Faith, Declaration regarding the Question of the Admission of Women to Ministerial Priesthood (*Inter Insigniores*), 1976, in *From "Inter Insigniores" to "Ordinatio Sacerdotalis": Documents and Commentaries*, 18–53 (Washington, DC: United States Catholic Conference, 1998), no. 4.

[24] See, e.g., *Women and Priesthood: Future Directions, A Call to Dialogue*, ed. Carroll Stuhlmueller, CP (Collegeville, MN: Liturgical Press, 1978).

[25] See J. Frank Henderson, "ICEL and Inclusive Language," in *Shaping English Liturgy: Studies in Honor of Archbishop Denis Hurley*, ed. Peter Finn and James Schellman (Washington, DC: The Pastoral Press, 1990), 272–73.

[26] Stated in response to a question during "A Conversation with Bishop Trautman," sponsored by the Georgetown Center for Liturgy as it celebrated its twenty-fifth anniversary on December 8, 2006.

[27] Congregation for Divine Worship and the Discipline of the Sacraments, Use of Female Altar Servers Allowed, *Origins* 23, no. 45 (April 28, 1994): 777, 779.

[28] John Paul II, *Ordinatio Sacerdotalis* (On Reserving Priestly Ordination to Men Alone), no. 4, http://www.vatican.va/holy_father/ john_paul_ii/apost_letters/documents/hf_jp-ii_apl_22051994_ordinatio-sacerdotalis_en.html.

[29] John Paul II, Letter to Women, *Origins* 25, no. 9 (July 27, 1995): 137, 139–43. For a more developed presentation of John Paul II's teaching on women, see John Paul II, *Mulieris Dignitatem* (On the Dignity and Vocation of Women), http://www.vatican.va/holy_father/john_paul_ii/apost_letters/documents/hf_jp-ii_apl_15081988_mulieris-dignitatem_en.html.

[30] John Paul II, Letter to Women, no. 11.

[31] See, e.g., Scott Alessi, "Fighting Back for Female Altar Servers," *U.S. Catholic*, November 23, 2011, http://www.uscatholic.org/blog/2011/11/fighting-back-female-altar-servers.

[32] Congregation for the Doctrine of the Faith, Letter to the Bishops of the Catholic Church on the Collaboration of Men and Women in the Church and in the World, 2004, http://www.vatican.va/roman_curia/congregations/cfaith/documents/rc_con_cfaith_doc_20040731_collaboration_en.html.

[33] Cf. article 5 and article 6 in Congregation for the Doctrine of the Faith, *Normae de Gravioribus Delictis,* May 21, 2010, http://www.vatican.va/resources/resources_norme_en.html.

[34] Tom Roberts, "Canon Lawyer Questions Maryknoll's Move against Bourgeois," *National Catholic Reporter*, September 14, 2011, http://ncronline.org/news/people/canon-lawyer-questions-maryknolls-move-against-bourgeois.

[35] David Todd Whitmore, "The Reception of Catholic Approaches to Peace and War in the United States," in *Modern Catholic Social Teaching: Commentaries and Interpretations*, ed. Kenneth Himes, OFM (Washington, DC: Georgetown University Press, 2006), 501–6.

[36] Drew Christiansen, SJ, "Commentary on *Pacem in Terris* (Peace on Earth)," in *Modern Catholic Social Teaching*, 218–22.

[37] Cf. John XXIII, *Pacem in Terris* (Peace on Earth), 1963, in *Catholic Social Thought*, ed. O'Brien and Shannon, 137–70; and United Nations, Universal Declaration of Human Rights, http://www.un.org/en/documents/udhr.

[38] U.S. Catholic Bishops, The Challenge of Peace: God's Promise and Our Response, in *Catholic Social Thought*, ed. O'Brien and Shannon, 492–571.

[39] See *Peacebuilding: Catholic Theology, Ethics, and Praxis,* ed. Robert J. Schreiter, R. Scott Appleby, and Gerard F. Powers (Maryknoll, NY: Orbis Books, 2010).

[40] Margaret A. Farley, "The Church in the Public Forum: Scandal or Prophetic Witness?" in *The Catholic Church, Morality and Politics*, ed. Charles E. Curran and Leslie Griffin (New York: Paulist Press, 2001), 208.

[41] David Hollenbach, "Joy and Hope, Grief and Anguish: *Gaudium et spes* 40 Years Later," *America*, December 5, 2005, 12–14.

[42] While the term "pro-life movement" began as an affirmative name for a movement labeled by its opponents as anti-abortion, I will use the term in the plural to consider movements opposed to capital punishment, euthanasia, and abortion, the three life issues that receive the greatest attention in *Evangelium Vitae*.

[43] See James F. Keenan, "The Moral Argumentation of *Evangelium Vitae*," in *Choosing Life: A Dialogue on* Evangelium Vitae, ed. Kevin Wm. Wildes, SJ, and Alan C. Mitchell (Washington, DC: Georgetown University Press, 1997), 48–52.

[44] Peter Black, CSsR, "Do Circumstances Ever Justify Capital Punishment?" *Theological Studies* 60 (1999): 338–45.

[45] For more on assisted suicide and the law, see M. Cathleen Kaveny, "Assisted Suicide, Euthanasia, and the Law," *Theological Studies* 58 (1997): 124–48.

[46] M. Cathleen Kaveny, "Intrinsic Evil and Political Responsibility: Is the Concept of Intrinsic Evil Helpful to Catholic Voters?" *America*, October 27, 2008, 15–19.

[47] See Thomas A. Shannon and James J. Walter, "The PVS Patient and the Forgoing/Withdrawing of Medical Nutrition and Hydration," *Theological Studies* 49 (1988): 623–47; Thomas A. Shannon and James J. Walter, "Assisted Nutrition and Hydration and the Catholic Church," *Theological Studies* 66 (2005): 651–62; and John J. Paris, James F. Keenan, and Kenneth R. Himes, "Did John Paul II's Allocution on Life-Sustaining Treatments Revise Tradition? A Response to Thomas A. Shannon and James J. Walter," *Theological Studies* 67 (2006): 163–68.

[48] Congregation for the Doctrine of the Faith, Responses to Certain Questions of the United States Conference of Catholic Bishops Concerning Artificial Nutrition and Hydration, August 2007, http://www.vatican.va/roman_curia/congregations/cfaith/documents/rc_con_cfaith_doc_20070801_risposte-usa_en.html.

[49] Suzanne Staggenborg, *The Pro-Choice Movement: Organization and Activism in the Abortion Conflict* (New York: Oxford University Press, 1991) 3, 9.

[50] Mary Ann Glendon, *Abortion and Divorce in Western Law: American Failures, European Challenges* (Cambridge, MA: Harvard University Press, 1987), 10–62.

[51] Ibid.

[52] Paul VI, *Populorum Progressio* (On the Development of Peoples), 1967, in *Catholic Social Thought*, ed. O'Brien and Shannon, p. 248, no. 37.

[53] Paul VI, *Humanae Vitae* (On the Regulation of Birth), 1968, no. 14, http://www.vatican.va/holy_father/paul_vi/encyclicals/documents/ hf_p-vi_enc_25071968_humanae-vitae_en.html.

[54] Congregation for the Doctrine of the Faith, Declaration on Procured Abortion, 1974, http://www.vatican.va/roman_curia/congregations/cfaith/ documents/rc_con_cfaith_doc_19741118_declaration-abortion_en.html.

[55] Pius XI, *Casti Connubii* (On Christian Marriage), 1930, http://www .vatican.va/holy_father/pius_xi/encyclicals/documents/hf_p-xi_enc_ 31121930_casti-connubii_en.html.

[56] Congregation for the Doctrine of the Faith, Instruction on Respect for Human Life in Its Origin and on the Dignity of Procreation: Replies to Certain Questions of the Day, 1987, http://www.vatican.va/roman_curia/congregations/ cfaith/documents/rc_con_cfaith_doc_19870222_respect-for-human -life_en.html; and Congregation for the Doctrine of the Faith, Letter to Bishops of the Catholic Church on the Pastoral Care of Homosexual Persons, 1986, no. 3, http://www.vatican.va/roman_curia/congregations/cfaith/documents/ rc_con_cfaith_doc_19861001_homosexual-persons_en.html.

[57] For theological reflection calling for change on this topic, see Kenneth R. Himes, OFM, and James A. Coriden, "The Indissolubility of Marriage: Reasons to Reconsider," *Theological Studies* 65 (2004): 454–99.

[58] Aidan McGrath, "The Problem of Scandal and Canon Law," *Priests & People* 17, no. 3 (March 2003): 111–15. *The Code of Canon Law: A Text and Commentary*, ed. James A. Coriden, Thomas J. Green, and Donald E. Heinschel (New York: Paulist Press, 1985).

[59] Keenan, "The Moral Argumentation of *Evangelium Vitae*," 48–52.

[60] Richard A. McCormick, SJ, *The Critical Calling: Reflections on Moral Dilemmas since Vatican II* (Washington, DC: Georgetown University Press, 2006), 121.

[61] Charles E. Curran, *Directions in Fundamental Moral Theology* (Notre Dame, IN: University of Notre Dame Press, 1985), 276.

[62] Richard McBrien, *Caesar's Coin: Religion and Politics in America* (New York: Macmillan, 1987), 155–57.

[63] Farley, "The Church in the Public Forum," 208.

Chapter 5—pages 85–97

[1] Kristen E. Heyer, *Prophetic and Public: The Social Witness of U.S. Catholicism* (Washington, DC: Georgetown University Press, 2006).

[2] David Todd Whitmore, "The Reception of Catholic Approaches to Peace and War in the United States," in *Modern Catholic Social Teaching: Commentaries and*

Interpretations, ed. Kenneth Himes (Washington, DC: Georgetown University Press, 2006), 515–16.

[3] The first statement was titled The Church in the 1976 Election. Since the United States Conference of Catholic Bishops chose not to issue a new statement in the fall of 2011 but rather to reaffirm their prior statement, the most recent is the 2007 statement, Forming Consciences for Faithful Citizenship. For an analysis of these, see Angela Senander, "Catholic Identity, *Faithful Citizenship*, and the Laity," in *Catholic Identity and the Laity*, ed. Timothy P. Muldoon, Annual Publication of the College Theology Society, vol. 54 (Maryknoll, NY: Orbis Books, 2009), 169–81.

[4] Congregation for the Doctrine of the Faith, Doctrinal Note on Some Questions Regarding the Participation of Catholics in Political Life, in *Readings on Catholics in Political Life*, ed. Task Force on Catholic Bishops and Catholic Politicians (Washington, DC: United States Conference of Catholic Bishops, 2006), 99–110.

[5] *Catechism of the Catholic Church*, 2nd edition (Washington, DC: United States Conference of Catholic Bishops, 2000), no. 2286.

[6] Mary Ann Glendon, *Abortion and Divorce in Western Law* (Cambridge, MA: Harvard University Press, 1987), 165.

[7] Ibid., 25–33.

[8] Ibid., 146–47.

[9] John Paul II, Letter to the Bishops of the German Episcopal Conference, 1998, http://www.vatican.va/holy_father/john_paul_ii/letters/1998/documents/hf_jp-ii_let_19980111_bishop-germany_en.html.

[10] "Kampfansage aus Rom," *Der Spiegel*, January 26, 1998, http://www.spiegel.de/spiegel/print/d-7809512.html.

[11] John Paul II, "An Unambiguous Witness to Human Life," *L'Osservatore Romano* (English edition), June 30, 1999, 2.

[12] Congregation for the Doctrine of the Faith, Doctrinal Note on Some Questions Regarding the Participation of Catholics in Political Life, 103.

[13] Raymond L. Burke, "Prophecy for Justice: Catholic Politicians and Bishops," *America*, June 21–28, 2004, 14.

[14] John A. McHugh, OP, and Charles J. Callan, OP, *Moral Theology: A Complete Course Based on St. Thomas Aquinas and the Best Modern Authorities*, vol. 1, revised by Edward P. Farrell, OP (New York City: Joseph F. Wagner, Inc., 1958), 609–10.

[15] Burke articulates his canonical reasoning in this matter in "The Discipline Regarding the Denial of Holy Communion to Those Obstinately Persevering in Manifest Grave Sin," *Periodica de Re Canonica* 96 (2007): 3–58.

[16] Cardinal William Keeler, "Summary of Consultations," in Interim Reflections of the Task Force on Catholic Bishops and Catholic Politicians, *Origins* 34, no. 7 (2004): 106.

[17] Archbishop William Levada, "Reflections on Catholics in Political Life and the Reception of Holy Communion," in Interim Reflections of the Task Force on Catholic Bishops and Catholic Politicians, 104–5.

[18] Synod of Bishops, Overview of the Synod's Propositions, *Origins* 35, no. 21 (2005): 348.

[19] Congregation for the Doctrine of the Faith, Doctrinal Note on Some Questions Regarding the Participation of Catholics in Political Life, 103, 106.

[20] United States Conference of Catholic Bishops, Happy Are Those Who Are Called to His Supper: On Preparing to Receive Christ Worthily in the Eucharist, 2006, 10–12, http://www.usccb.org/about/doctrine/publications.

[21] When officials at the 1996 Republican National Convention directed William Weld to speak only about economics in his address, he decided not to address the convention. See "Republican Moderates Speak Out on Abortion," *AllPolitics*, CNN/Time, August 12, 1996, http://cgi.cnn.com/ALLPOLITICS/1996/news/9608/12/abortion.rally/index.shtml. See also Robert P. Casey, *Fighting for Life* (Dallas: Word Publishing, 1996), 177–92.

[22] John P. Beal, "Holy Communion and Unholy Politics," *America*, June 21, 2004, 16–18.

[23] Michael Sheridan, A Pastoral Letter to the Catholic Faithful of the Archdiocese of Colorado Springs on the Duties of Catholic Politicians and Voters, May 1, 2004, http://www.diocs.org/About/BishopSheridan/PastoralLetters/PastoralLetter01May2004.aspx.

[24] "Cardinal Ratzinger Addresses the Issue of Holy Communion for Pro-abortion Catholic Politicians," *Origins* 34, no. 8 (July 15, 2004): 114. The significance of the Communion controversy for the US Catholic Church is highlighted in David Hollenbach's reflection on the politics of abortion in the 2004 election, when he named it as a sign of the times from North America for Catholic theological ethicists from around the world during his plenary presentation at the Catholic Theological Ethics in the World Church conference in 2006. See David Hollenbach, SJ, "Catholic Ethics in a World Church: A U.S. View," in *Catholic Theological Ethics in the World Church: The Plenary Papers from the First Cross-Cultural Conference on Catholic Theological Ethics*, ed. James F. Keenan, SJ (New York: Continuum, 2007), 140–46.

[25] United States Conference of Catholic Bishops, Catholics in Political Life, 2004, 214.

[26] John Noonan, "Address at Notre Dame Commencement," *Origins* 39, no. 4 (June 4, 2009): 53–54.

[27] "Tough Crowd! But Seriously, Folks . . ." *South Bend Tribune*, April 23, 2006, http://articles.southbendtribune.com/2006-04-23/news/26930011_1_zeus-students-speaker.

[28] Jennifer Jacobson, "2 Professors at Boston College Protest Honorary Degree for Condoleezza Rice," *The Chronicle of Higher Education*, May 4, 2006, http://chronicle.com/article/2-Professors-at-Boston-College/118118; and Hollenbach, "Catholic Ethics in a World Church," 140.

[29] Jacobson, "2 Professors at Boston College Protest Honorary Degree for Condoleezza Rice."

[30] Congregation for the Doctrine of the Faith, Doctrinal Note on Some Questions Regarding the Participation of Catholics in Political Life, 107.

[31] Gerald Kelly, SJ, *Medico-Moral Problems* (St. Louis, MO: The Catholic Hospital Association of the United States and Canada, 1958), 226.

[32] Clarke E. Cochran, "Catholic Health Care and the Challenge of Civic Society," in *American Catholics and Civic Engagement: A Distinctive Voice*, American Catholics in the Public Square, ed. Margaret O'Brien Steinfels, vol. 1 (Lanham, MD: Rowman & Littlefield Publishers, Inc., 2004), 126–44.

[33] For references to scandal in the most recent edition, see United States Conference of Catholic Bishops, Ethical and Religious Directives for Catholic Health Care Services, 5th ed., 2009, pp. 26, 35–37, 42, http://usccb.org/issues-and-action/human-life-and-dignity/health-care/upload/Ethical-Religious-Directives-Catholic-Health-Care-Services-fifth-edition-2009.pdf. For historical perspectives, see James F. Keenan, SJ, "Institutional Cooperation and the Ethical and Religious Directives," *Linacre Quarterly* 64 (August 1997): 53–72; Kevin D. O'Rourke, "The Ethical and Religious Directives: History, Content, and Difficulties," *Canon Law Society of America Proceedings*, 65 (2003): 171–80.

[34] NETWORK, "Catholic Sisters' Letter in Support of Healthcare Reform Bill," 2010, http://www.networklobby.org/legislation/catholic-sisters-letter-support-healthcare-reform-bill.

[35] Joan Frawley Desmond, "A 'Catholic' Social Justice Lobby?" *National Catholic Register*, April 19, 2010, http://www.ncregister.com/daily-news/a_catholic_social_justice_lobby/.

[36] See M. Therese Lysaught, "Moral Analysis of Procedure at Phoenix Hospital," *Origins* 40, no. 33 (January 27, 2011): 537–49; Bishop Thomas Olmsted, "Phoenix Hospital No Longer Considered Catholic," *Origins* 40, no. 31 (January 13, 2011): 505–7; St. Joseph's Hospital and Medical Center, "Q and A on Phoenix Hospital's Status," *Origins* 40, no. 31 (January 13, 2011): 507–9; National Catholic Bioethics Center, "Commentary on the Phoenix Hospital Situation," *Origins* 40, no. 33 (January 27, 2011): 549–51; Kevin O'Rourke, "What Happened in Phoenix? The Complicated Reasons behind an Abortion at a Catholic Hospital," *America*, June 21, 2010, http://www.americamagazine.org/content/article.cfm?article_id=12348; Kevin O'Rourke, "Complications: A Catholic Hospital, a Pregnant Mother and a Questionable Excommunication," *America*, August 2–9, 2010, 15–16; and Kevin O'Rourke, "From Intuition to Moral Principle: Examining the Phoenix Case in Light of Church Tradition," *America*, November 15, 2010, 11–14.

[37] Thomas Wenski, "Archbishop Wenski: On Healthcare, Protect 'Rights of Conscience,'" *Miami Herald*, December 2, 2011, http://www.miamiherald.com/2011/12/02/2529212/archbishop-wenski-on-healthcare.html.

Index